MY F

&

THE LOST LEGEND OF PEAR TREE

PART ONE

'A hugely important story, told with profound, sometimes painful honesty regarding a subject we all too readily shy away from. Kalwinder Singh Dhindsa captures the vibrancy, the reality, the complexity of every Punjabi family. And he shares the tragedy of his own. A brave and captivating read'

Hardeep Singh Kohli

'Anyone who has been stalked by the Black Dog, anyone who has had the shadows and tragedies of life growl at them, will recognize the brave brutal truth of this work. Kalwinder Singh Dhindsa moves with unexpected grace from the darkest places to cathartic moments of joy and insight. More sorrow, drama and redemption per page than I have read for a long time.

This is a voyage connecting Derby, India and the worlds of Doctor Who through all the stations of the human heart'

David Southwell

Part Two
THE CREST
Kalwinder Singh Dhindsa

'I fell in love with a Stainsby girl'

Cover design by Tamás Miklós Fülep

@TomFulep
www.fulep.com

Edited by Fine Point Editing

@FP_Editing
www.finepointediting

Copyright © 2018 by Kalwinder Singh Dhindsa

All rights reserved

The right of Kalwinder Singh Dhindsa to be identified as the author of this work has been asserted by him in accordance with the Copyright, Designs and Patents Act, 1988.

This book or any portion thereof may not be reproduced or used in any manner whatsoever without the express written permission of the publisher except for the use of brief quotations in a book review.

First Printing, 2018

ISBN-10: 1986351769 (PRINT)
ISBN-13: 978-1986351768 (PRINT)

@KhalSir

@PearTreeDerby

www.khalsir.com

Year 2
John Port School

Chapter 13: Seconds

It was Monday, September 4th 2006 and life was not great. Today was an INSET day and tomorrow would be the first day of another academic year.

It had been a whole year since I first began teaching as an NQT Science Teacher at John Port School in Etwall, Derbyshire. I was now a fully fledged qualified teacher. What a year it had been. My NQT year was behind me. I had survived. Surely things would be easier this year - the second time around?

I quickly discovered that some things remained the same; I continued to experience the same problems with misbehaviour and poor attitudes towards learning. Nothing seemed to have changed on the surface for the better. The light at the end of the tunnel once again began to disappear into the distance. I had also been given some extra responsibilities. A sixth form tutor group and some additional dinnertime duties.

My own school days at the Village Community School were so much more pleasant on the discipline front. I had it easy at school. My good friend Richard Do was a bright and intelligent student born to immigrant Vietnamese parents. He was just like me in the sense that we both wanted to do well academically at school. Rich also had a reputation as someone who could look after himself and someone not to mess with. He could also have days when he acted up but when he wanted to put his head down and work he made sure the whole class followed suit. Thus, any trouble making from silly individuals would result in a slow turn of his head followed by a cold lingering stare that would nip any misbehaviour in the bud, instantly. The scolded child would then nod sheepishly to appease Rich, as discipline would be restored. He would then catch my eye, wink and smile.

School life was grinding me down again. The growling black dog had returned by my side and there was nothing I could do but submit to it and remain silent. I was stuck between a rock and a hard place. I really had no one to talk to about the difficulties I was experiencing as I progressively began to distance myself from my friends and family. It was not a deliberate act, but deep down I began to think that nobody would want to talk to me because I would only be bringing them down with me if I engaged in talk about my father.

My life was becoming increasingly more and more isolated from the real world. I just wanted to be alone. I just wanted to be at home. I would spend so much time over the school week shouting, but then spend weekends in silence. It began to feel as if I had no life and no future to look forward to any more. Weekends would be spent entirely in silence on the Internet keeping an eye on the footy scores to see how I was doing in the fantasy football league or Wiki surfing.

Wiki surfing was the act of going from one Wikipedia article to another by right clicking over a link and then opening that new link in a new tab. For example, I might have been interested in the town of Ilkeston and as I read through the article I then began opening separate tabs on the River Erewash, Domesday Book, Robert Lindsay and so on. And I would keep doing this until I had about 30 new tabs open above my address bar that would only disappear once I had read the article and then exited from it. This activity was obviously highly time consuming, but in the long run it kept me distracted and the more time I gave to it the more I learned about the world I lived in and also the connections to my own birth place of Derby.

I would also keep myself busy by buying random stuff from

eBay and other gadget based online retailers. It was a way to keep my spirits up. Buying things I never had when I was a child to keep me happy. They were like little highs for me that resulted in small victories. I would bid for them on eBay or buy them outright from online stores, then bring them into school to show off to the students. Most of these things had some kind of scientific connection, i.e. Yo-Yos, Slinkies, Thinking Putty etc. It was almost as if I was trying to reclaim a lost childhood and hoarding as many little memories of it together as I could. To remember happier days in my life; happier days with my father by my side and still alive.

When I was a child I would cut out from the Argos catalogue pictures of toys that I wanted. I would then place them in my shirt pocket and sometimes show them to my father in the hope he would buy them for me. I once had my heart set on a He-Man action figure. He-Man was a playground hero for us all at Pear Tree Infants and we never ever missed an episode of the animated television series 'He-Man and the Masters of the Universe'. On one Saturday morning my father took me into town with him. As we entered the Argos store in the main centre, he asked me for my cut out picture. He then passed it over to one of the cashiers. I looked on, at the empty shelves. 'What were all these people queuing up for?', I wondered to myself. 'There's nothing in this store. Nor will there be any

He-Man action figures'. I could only hope, my father had tried his best for me in his broken English. A few minutes later the cashier returned with a small package and my father paid for it. He then handed it over to me with a smile. I couldn't believe it as I pulled it out the carrier bag. It was a brand new shiny 'He-Man – Flying Fists' action figure in its original packaging. I didn't have many toys when I was growing up so I guarded He-Man with my life. I would literally not let go of him at bedtime – only after I was fast asleep would my mother be able to prise him out of my hands.

As the new academic year went on the same thoughts and feelings from the previous year began to consume my thoughts again. I should have been teaching but I just could not stop thinking about my father and all that I had lost. There was absolutely nothing I could do to reclaim his physical loss. However, something I could reclaim was what he had left behind – but what? 'What did he leave you?', I kept asking myself. He had to have left something. He didn't live for nothing. He didn't die for nothing. He had a purpose and I knew I had to reclaim that purpose to allow myself to live again.

During these periods of darkness there was one thing I always managed to happily distract myself with. Thinking about my past would stir up so many happy memories. The memories that I had retained were a great painkiller to keep my spirits up, even more so, when many of those memories were also attached to my father. Gradually they became a therapy against the black dog that was still by my side. I guess in this sense I was living again, albeit in the past.

The continuing problems at school regularly brought me down and to top it off I was now doing dinner duty from Monday to Friday for half an hour each day. My NQT supervisor from the previous year had suggested that it might be a good idea – to allow me to build better relationships and get to know the children better.

It initially turned out to be an awful experience; I became the last line of defence before the children would make their way into the dining hall. It was my job to make sure that all the children were lined up sensibly, having placed their bags and coats neatly on the shelves and coat hooks either side of them when entering the corridor. I would then be able to allow small groups of them to enter the dining hall on the instruction of a dinner lady who stood close to the entrance of the dining hall.

It would never transpire like this though. What would actually happen is that everyday I would be greeted by hordes of hungry children who would stampede through the corridor to try and get to the front of the queue first. No attention was paid to placing their bags and rucksacks carefully on the shelves and hooks provided. Nor was any attention paid to lining up sensibly. Instead, many of the bags and rucksacks would be thrown all over the ground. It was an absolute nightmare and very dangerous for all the other children entering the corridor later on. There was very little I could do on my own when the children behaved like this. On occasions a dinner lady would try to help but she was point blank ignored and treated very rudely and disrespectfully.

The vast majority of these early arrivals were also the naughty and hyperactive ones to boot and it was my responsibility to tame them. The only way I could do this was to raise my voice and shout at them when they became too rowdy and disobedient. Their hunger pains obviously added to their temporal wildness. I felt so sorry for the dinner ladies and midday supervisors and the abuse they would receive. I also felt very sorry for the well-behaved children who would be jostled and intimidated whilst patiently waiting to enter the dining hall. It was all becoming quite painful to have to bear.

On one occasion a child stormed through the corridor as others were sensibly waiting and forcibly barged his way through the queue, knocking children all over the place like a wrecking ball. It was too late to shout and berate him so as soon as he rushed past me I grabbed him by the handle of his rucksack, pulled him back and then swung him around to face me. Back of the line!

It was a horrible situation to find myself in day after day, when all I needed was a break from the classroom and to be able to relax for a bit. Instead it just resulted in me becoming constantly annoyed and frustrated with the lack of discipline in the school and the relative inaction when things were reported. It really became a hell's kitchen for me, but I tried to stick it out for as long as I could. After all, it would help with building relationships, so I was told.

I carried on with this duty for about 3 months in total. Having initially began on 5 days a week then dropping down to 3 days a week. Thankfully not long after that I was transferred to outside duties. I guess the amount of complaints I was making about bad behaviour must have annoyed management, so they moved me somewhere else.

Once outside, things really did improve for me and I did find that I got to know the children better. It was great chatting to them all in a more relaxed atmosphere away from the stresses and strains of the classroom and corridors. I even got to know some of the silly ones better. They seemed more friendlier and approachable outside than when they were in the classroom.

During these duties, I once again found myself having no time whatsoever to eat as I was still trying to use any free time I had to prepare for the lessons ahead. The anxieties and panic that resulted once again began to slowly make their way back into my life, just as they had done in the previous year.

There's always Hope, I used to tell myself. In my Year 9 teaching group, there was a student called Hope. She had begun the year a bit disillusioned and unhappy, but as time went on she started to come more and more out of her shell as she continued to rack up some very good marks in her end-of-topic tests. It was a pleasure to see her smile as her confidence grew over time. It always made me happy to see her continued progress, as it also became a beautiful reminder to me. No matter how bad things get, there is always hope.

Another way that I used to get over the dark periods in my life at school was talk about things in class that made me happy or that I associated with happiness. Sometimes they would not even be science related but I would try to weave them into conversation at every opportunity I could.

On one particular day during a rare quiet moment whilst teaching my Year 9's, I was talking about Brian Clough and Derby County F.C. when a couple of voices in the back of the science lab began to laugh and then mockingly call out the name of one of the students in the front row. One of the voices then said 'Jonny's Dad played for Derby County Sir'. I looked towards the front bench and noticed Jon bow his head and then mutter, 'He broke his leg, Sir'. My jaw dropped – I looked down at him as I tried to consider what had just been revealed to me. 'Jon, Jon Taylor', I reminded myself. Within a split second I had realised that Jon was the son of former Derby County F.C. goalkeeper, Martin Taylor.

'Oh my goodness', I thought to myself as my mind was momentarily taken back to the day I was at the Baseball Ground to see his father being awarded the 1993–94 Jack Stamps Player of the Year Trophy. 'I know your dad', I replied with a smile. Jon was now looking down at the floor, kicking at the football in his carrier bag that he always had with him.

Martin Taylor was one of my all time Rams heroes for what he achieved in his career. He had indeed broken his leg the following season after his Player of the Year trophy at Derby County F.C. It did not end his career though, he came back from his leg break and resurrected his career at Wycombe Wanderers. A club he joined on loan at the end of the 1996– 97 season. He went on to miss just seven league games in four seasons, culminating a clean sweep of the Player of the Season awards in May 2001. This followed a season where he was not only ever-present with a staggering 63 appearances but also achieved hero status during the record breaking FA Cup run. The 5th round replay at Selhurst Park on Tuesday, February 20th 2001 was an evening that would never be forgotten for Taylor and the Wycombe fans who were there. Taylor saved a penalty in the last minute of normal time and then scored from the spot in the penalty shoot-out.

As all these memories of Martin Taylor came flooding back to me I looked back at Jon and my first thought was that I had embarrassed him. For a moment, I honestly thought he was embarrassed by his father. 'I was there at the Baseball Ground the day he was awarded Derby County's Player of the Season award, Jon'. Jon looked up and smiled. I realised that it wasn't embarrassment that Jon was feeling when he bowed his head, it was absolute pride in his father. It was the same prickly pride I had felt all those years ago in my history lesson when Mr Montgomery told my class about the contribution of Sikh soldiers during two world wars. To remember that same feeling of pride reawakened my spirits. But this time it managed to manifest in a father–son relationship. Having lost my father I knew how important moments like these were in young children's lives.

Later on in the day I bumped into Jon again and showed him some printouts about his father's career exploits. We also talked about Wycombe Wanderer's amazing FA Cup run of 2001 and the final game against Liverpool F.C. A game in which his father had played so determinedly for so long, trying to keep out the likes of Robbie Fowler, Emile Heskey and Michael Owen.

A few weeks later I met Jon and his father at a Year 9 parents' evening. It was an honour to talk to Martin Taylor and discuss Jon's progress. At the end of the appointment I shook Martin's hand and asked for his autograph, which he happily signed for me. I was filled with joy. Jon's father had always been a great hero in my eyes; he had played for Derby County F.C. just like the legendary Steve Bloomer of England.

Jon was obviously very proud of what his father had achieved in life. It thus reaffirmed within me what I already knew, that I too should always be very proud of my own father.

As the academic year went on I began building better relationships with the students. For the first time in a long time I began seeing them as children who also had parents. Parents who only ever wanted the best for their child, to see them flourish and achieve. But, deep down I always knew that I had to be extra careful as to how much of my true self I revealed to them. After all, the last thing I wanted was for the students to know or even find out what had happened to my father and how he had tragically died.

On a few occasions I was asked what my real name was. The students already knew my initials as KSD so they would playfully guess as to what the K stood for. I never kept the S for Singh a secret as I was always open and honest about being a Derby born Punjabi Sikh. But, just to play along with their games I would tell them that the KS really stood for Keyser Söze, the main antagonist in the film *The Usual Suspects*.

Unfortunately, my contrived efforts to keep my family life a secret from the children were well and truly scuppered when my brother began running a shop around the corner from school, which he had leased. In no time at all the students had discovered that he was my brother. Their suspicions had arisen due to the similarity in our facial features. I didn't know if he had told them outright or if they just worked it out themselves, but soon after random students began asking me if I had a brother who worked at the shop around the corner. Initially, I didn't know anything about him working there, so I just denied all knowledge of it. It was only when I one day asked my mother after work that I found he had indeed been working at that shop. This made things in the classroom even more difficult when students began questioning me about whether he was my brother. They also began passing on information they had gleaned from my brother to others.

My brother had put me in a very awkward position – my private life was now being openly discussed at school. Teaching was already a difficult job. I really didn't need to go home after a long day and hear from other family members what the children thought of me when my brother would then share these stories with them. It was just not on; my school and private life had to be kept separate. From then on, when the children did ask me about him I made it quite clear that I didn't have a brother and that they were mistaken. It was far too risky for me to let them into my private life. I had no other choice but to deny all knowledge of him. I didn't appreciate this act of pure stupidity and insensitivity from my brother. There was no way I was going to allow this intrusion of my privacy to be played out in my place of work. At that time I was not ready to discuss my father's death with anyone, never mind the way he had died, and even if I did want to discuss it, it would only have been with people I trusted 100%.

However, deep down I still wanted to talk about my father in the hope that he would continue to be remembered for the life he had lived and all the good that he had contributed. Suicide had stopped him from talking; suicide was now stopping me from talking about him. That was not fair. My father was a good man; he deserved not to be forgotten because of the way he had died.

Chapter 14: Operation DynaMo

A new long-term cover teacher joined the science department during the second academic year. From the moment I met Grace Young we got on very well with each other. I put this mainly down to the fact that she had a son called Robert who was the same age as me. Another reason for this could have been because she also had no idea as to who I was and what I had been through in my life over the last year or so. This made it even easier for me to engage with her knowing there would be no awkwardness between us regarding the suicide of my father.

One lunchtime I was sitting alone in the corner of the staffroom when Grace approached me and asked if she could join me. We then struck up a conversation about what our plans were for the Christmas period ahead. As she began telling me of her plans to spend some time in the Shetland Isles, something clicked in my mind, 'Shetland Isles, you say? I had a friend at school whose family were originally from there. His name was Rob'. As soon as I had said Rob the penny dropped, I knew this lady. 'Hold on, your Robert's Mum?' I excitedly called out. She smiled 'Yes, I am'.

I had first met Grace many years previously in the Pear Tree Juniors playground on Pear Tree Street. On that day myself, Rob and a couple of other friends were happily playing football with a tennis ball when we noticed an African lady walk through the school gates. I looked on at her beaming face, paying special attention to the Rastacap type hat she was wearing to keep all her hair in place. Upon seeing me she began to laugh out loud hysterically and then point her finger at me. 'He's got a little flowerpot on his head, isn't it beautiful?', she said as she placed her hand over her mouth to hide her amusement. I didn't know what to think or even say. I was completely stumped by her reaction towards me. I looked around at my friends who were now also laughing apart from one who looked even more embarrassed than me. Rob then shouted towards her as she walked towards the reception still smiling, 'It's called a topknot, Mum!'. It was obvious his mother had never seen a young Sikh with a topknot before. So I didn't take it to heart or even question that the word used to describe my topknot might be considered to be offensive to some people. And anyway on first impressions that definitely did not fit the jovial character she was displaying.

As soon as I realised that Grace was Rob's Mum I burst out laughing. I had not laughed like this in school for months, especially not with another member of staff. I explained to her how I knew her from the past and how Rob and I had been friends and how he used to share stories about his old life in the Shetlands with us all at school. I also mentioned to her where I still lived. At this point Grace began to smile. 'I know your Dad. I've not seen him for a long while. How is he?', she asked. I immediately stopped smiling. She seemed so happy talking about my father and I didn't want to break the tragic news to her. But I had to tell her the truth. 'He died Grace'. As soon as I said it, her smile evaporated and she became visibly saddened by my revelation. I then had to explain to her when my father had died and what led up to his death. Most importantly of all I had to reveal to her that my father had taken his own life. Suicide.

As we continued to talk I realised that speaking about my father didn't upset me as much as I thought it would because at the same time it also pleased me that she and my father had been friends. This realisation made me feel very happy. Grace told me about her memories of my father and what a nice man he was. How he would always acknowledge her and say hello whenever they met even if it was from afar. It was so lovely to hear this from her and also be able to make such a happy connection back to my past. But more than anything I was very grateful for this moment between us as for the first time since my father's death I had opened up at school about his death. I was finally beginning to come out of my shell.

In mid-2004 a childhood dream came true for me. I became the proud owner of a pair of South American Red Foot Tortoise. I had always wanted a Tortoise, ever since I saw my first real one, which belonged to a teacher at Pear Tree Infants. Reading Roald Dahl's Essio Trot during my time at Pear Tree Juniors would also have added to my desire to own one.

When I finally made the decision to purchase a tortoise I ended up getting two instead. I just could not bear keeping one on it's own in isolation. I named one of them Winston and the other Dahl. Winston was the black one and Dahl was the brown one. It was only after four years of growth that I was finally able to figure out what sex they were. I later found out that Winston was a male and Dahl was a female by checking the development of their plastron underneath their shells. Had I bought my Tortoise after the death of Brian

Clough on September 20th 2004, they would have no doubt been named Clough and Taylor.

Sir Winston Leonard Spencer-Churchill, Roald Dahl and Brian Howard Clough had always been great heroes of mine and to top it off they all had one thing they had in common that united them. The Royal Air Force. In my mind the RAF was the epitome of British resistance during World War II.

Sir Winston Leonard Spencer-Churchill as a wartime leader invigorated our nation with his speeches. Deploying the RAF to resist everything the Luftwaffe could throw at our brave and defiant nation against insurmountable odds.

Roald Dahl the great British children's author was also a fighter pilot in the RAF during the battle of Malta in World War II. It was also nice to know that we both shared the same birth date too, 13th September. I first came across Roald Dahl's books when Mr Owen read The Twits to our class in Pear Tree Juniors. I have loved the magical worlds that Roald Dahl created ever since.

Brian Clough also had a connection to the RAF. He originally left school in 1950 without any qualifications to work at ICI and then did his National Service in the RAF Regiment between 1953 and 1955.

Just before Christmas 2006 John Port School had an Ofsted Inspection. It was carried out over the 13–14 December 2006 and coincided, fortunately for the school, with the Year 11s being on study leave. I say fortunately because had the Ofsted Inspectors witnessed some of the behavior the Year 11s engaged in at times there would be no way the school would have got the report it eventually did. I was not observed myself but other teachers in the science department were.

Not long after the Ofsted Inspectors came in, the school received its overall report. This determined that the governance, leadership and management and value for money are outstanding. Students' behaviour was good and their attendance was high.

When the teachers were all informed about the report, and those two points in particular, many of us just couldn't believe what we were hearing. I immediately resigned myself to the fact that misbehaviour was not going to be tackled and improved on and that things would remain as they were. My spirits plummeted.

Even before the report came out, I knew that one of two things could happen regarding behaviour and discipline, either it would be mentioned and something would be done to radically change the school's approach or nothing at all is mentioned to raise any concerns. Sadly for me the latter occurred. It was quite obvious now, to the management; if it ain't broke don't fix it. Things were not going to get any better, I would have to struggle on. There just didn't seem to be any way out for me.

I desperately needed a way out, but I just could not see an open window. I had already been thinking about giving up the job even before Ofsted came in. But I had a Year-12 tutor group and wanted to see them out to the end of Year 13. I also wanted to do a five-year cycle, so I could at least say I stuck it out for five years. But all that seemed more and more unlikely after the Ofsted report.

As the days went on after the report was revealed, I continued to experience the same problems with misbehaving students and poor attitude towards learning. I began to start making plans for a tactical withdrawal. I initially talked to my colleague, Tim Fearn and we discussed it at length including the consequences of leaving my position and what I could do next. By now I had realised that enough was enough and sooner or later I had to move on. Things were not going to get any better in school.

I thought about my father. I had done him proud, but I was unhappy. The management just didn't listen to my concerns, they heard what I was saying, but they just did not back me up with the support I required. It was all just too frustrating. I felt sorry for the students that wanted to learn; time and time again, things were not followed up, no matter how much the science department and I tried to rectify things. The school was just too big for its own good. The left hand did not know what the right was doing. I was being pushed too far and expected to sort my problems out myself when at times the problems were more institutional rather than of my own making.

During my second year at John Port School, one thing that was always not far from my mind was the fast approaching one-year anniversary of my father's death. From the moment my father passed away I had been typing up my thoughts on my PDA device. It was the only way I could try to make sense of what had happened in my life. It was the only thing I truly engaged with about the unhappiness in my life.

Thursday, February 15th 2007 Diary Entry

It has nearly been a year now since my Da passed away. Still miss him terribly, every minute I think of him, sometimes I even have to preoccupy my mind with other things just to get by with not thinking about him and what happened. Times like this normally occur when I have time off from work like holidays. Well I decided in the last few weeks that this year will be my last teaching at this school. I need to move on, it is not doing me any good hanging about much longer, I need my life back. The longer I stay the worse it will become there. I've made my Da proud I stuck with it. I persevered, I survived, and I conquered. Time to move onto the next mission in life, to get back to life and carry his name with me to the next idea. Driving school; started the course last August but will begin it again in March and try and complete it by the end of this year. Should be out of JPS by mid-July, I've done my time. Will take March 1st off school, don't want to be there, maybe a couple of days off? At first it was ok being at school straight after but now I think the longer I am there the more my life is being taken away from me and my family. If only I could have taken that day off to help him?

Life is for living, I need to start living again, for me and my Da and my family.

Friday, February 16th 2007 Diary Entry

Can't sleep back to school in a couple of days, still got plenty of marking to do, will get most of it done. Still feeling down and depressed. A manic sort, real highs and then real lows. All this time off, too much time to think. That's why I am constantly on the net, reading, buying stuff. Keeps me occupied. What will happen, when I leave work? To be honest though I have always been like this, leaving things till the end and becoming anxious about it. So it is not entirely due to Da, I remember similar situations last year before all this happened. Guess I'm having a mild Robbie Williams effect, constantly looking for buzzes, small ones, ups and downs. Decided, should really take Wednesday and Thursday off maybe Friday? Maybe not? Even before Da went I have had the following thought; sometimes I wish I was dying at least then I would have something to live for. Need something to live for, I'm not saying I'm unhappy and miserable now, *but I need the carrot in front of me to persevere/pursue.*

Endurance will conquer. A child is required I think, a real one. Nintendogs will just not do, well maybe for a short period of time.

;)

To live for.... To make proud.
To die for, proud to be called the son.

When the day of the one-year anniversary of my father's death finally arrived, it coincided with a Year 10 parents' evening. I had already decided to take two days off, Wednesday, February 28th and Thursday, March 1st. I wanted to spend the days off at home with Rav and close to my mother. At the time I did not want to tell my students the real reason for my absence because I did not want to share my private life with them. On top of this I was also having a few problems with this particular science group. I had been trying my best for so long but things were just not going the way I had hoped. Some days were good but others not so. I did all I could with this group, but I was struggling and I needed help. Some assistance did eventually come my way but it didn't take long before things returned to as they were.

A few days before parents' evening, gossip got back to me that some students were suggesting that the reason I did not want to go to parents' evening was because I was afraid of meeting the parents. Members of staff had also told me that one or two parents had been asking why I wouldn't be attending.

When I next met my science group I decided to share with them my reasons for not wanting to attend. I had to be honest and I didn't want anyone thinking I was afraid. It had nothing to do with that. I just didn't want to be there. At the very end of the lesson I asked them all to be quiet, eventually they settled down to listen. I then said the following. 'Some of you will no doubt be wondering why I will not able to attend parents' evening on Thursday. Well this is my reason. On Wednesday, March 1st 2006, my father passed away'. Suddenly there was absolute silence, until I heard one student whisper to her friend beside her, 'he *died*?'. I smiled as I noticed her friend roll her eyes and then tell her, 'shhhh'. I had gotten all their attention now. 'The reason I will not attend parents' evening is because on that day one year previously at around 19:25 I was watching my father die as his life support machine was switched off. I watched him take his final breaths and that was it, my father died'. You could now hear a pin drop. 'Now if I attended parents' evening on Thursday at around the same time, the only thing on my mind would have been, this time last year I was in hospital watching my father die. He would have been taking his last breath now and so on. That is why I will not attend, I am sorry'.

I looked upon their stunned faces. I had to break the wall of silence. I smiled, 'that shut you up didn't it'. A burst of laughter put them all at ease again as the bell then rang for the end of the lesson.

After my revelation to the group my relationship with them improved for the better. I still had some off days, but I liked them, and I would like to think that many of them liked me too.

Thursday, March 1st 2007 Diary Entry

One year over, no more this time last year. But the anniversaries would still come.

I carried on the best I could after the one-year anniversary but I had all but decided my future at the school. Two incidents in particular occurred which really unsettled me and made me question whether I was in the right job or not at all.

On one occasion I was making my way into the main science block carrying two heavy boxes of textbooks as well as my rucksack. I was carrying far more than I should have in the process of trying to save time and not make two trips to my next lesson. Just as I was making my way into the building, a large number of students were also trying to make their way out of the block using the same doors. As I was a teacher I had hoped that a few of them would see that I was carrying a heavy load and naturally step aside for me and prop the door open to let me in. But not one student stopped or even looked up to see me coming towards them. So I waited for a couple of seconds and when there was a large enough gap I attempted to go through the door. However, just at that moment a young student had also tried to exit the building as I tried to enter it from the same door. This resulted in me having to stop and almost drop the boxes and my rucksack. I then lost my temper in frustration and raised my voice at her, 'Oh come on! Give me a break'. Only then was I given a bit of space to make my way into the building. However, as soon as I entered the building I instantly regretted losing my temper, as the student I had raised my voice to had not blocked my path intentionally. She just was not paying attention. She was a pleasant student who I had regularly seen around school. As soon as I realised this I began to feel sorry for her and the upset I may have caused. I wanted to apologise later on but was unable to find her again. Maybe she began to avoid me from then on. I really felt disappointed in myself for snapping at her as it was not the person I truly was or wanted to be. But it was obvious that all the pressures of life and school life were gradually beginning to wear me down and get the better of me.

Another incident that brought out the frustration in me involved a student in my Year 10 group.

Now this particular student was an intelligent enough pupil for him to be in a higher ability science group. It's just that on most occasions he was just not interested in doing any work at all in lesson. It was obvious that his mind was preoccupied with other things and he had a temper on him that would result in him exploding in rage if he felt that he was being confronted. From my first meeting with him I was made aware that he had some issues that were playing heavily on his mind. So I always tried my best not to antagonise him; I didn't want to upset him any further.

Now I could totally accept his predicament as I found myself in the same position at school with my own personal life. Sometimes he would be no problem in lesson and would happily get on with his work and engage. Other times he would just switch off and sit in his place doodling on the piece of paper I had given to him because he had forgotten to bring his exercise book. Now in all honesty, when I could see he was not switched on I would just let him get on with it. The science group he was in had a few other characters that would try to play up in lesson regularly. So I turned a blind eye to his quiet doodling; one less student to worry about. On the whole though we both got on reasonably well.

As the months went on during the second academic year, this Year 10 group began to provide me with growing problems and become a bit of a handful, although there were just as many students in the class that were well behaved and hardworking. Once again I tried to fill in referral forms and nothing was being done by the management to help me improve the class's overall attitude and behavior. So, again I was left to my own devices knowing full well I would be getting myself in more and more trouble with the management if I didn't deal with the problems myself. I had been trying for weeks to get this particular group in some kind of order while not having the support of management, but these issues were not very well dealt with. I had regularly told the group of my concerns with their general attitude and behaviour, especially considering that they had some very important exams ahead of them. So what happened? Well, things just got worse until one day things came to a head, quite literally.

During one lesson there had been a room change and as the group entered the lab, the students came in and sat down wherever they could find a space. As we had already wasted so much time, I just let them sit where they were and not move them about again. There was an important end-of-topic test coming up and I was already quite stressed and anxious trying my best to make them all pay attention and concentrate on what I was teaching them.

A few minutes into the lesson, I had been talking away at the front of the lab in my elevated position when I noticed that one particular student was having his own conversation with the person sitting next to him, not paying the slightest bit of attention to what I was saying. So I stopped speaking and then asked him to stop talking and pay attention. But he carried on talking and completely ignored me. I asked him again to stop talking and pay attention. Once again he ignored me and carried on. This really infuriated me. I felt he was now blatantly disrespecting me and I was not going to have it. I raised my voice at him and told him 'if you don't want to be here then you might as well go outside, as you're not learning anything in here'. He carried on talking. 'Right outside' I shouted. At this point he threw down the pen he was holding and slammed it into the bench. He stood up and began making his way to the front of the class whilst muttering something inaudible. As he made his way around the front bench I stepped down from the elevated platform I was standing on and then moved towards him to make sure that he knew I was serious and that I wanted him out. He obviously saw this as a confrontation and leaned into me on his way out with his head. Just as he passed he brought his head towards mine and as I was already moving forward I moved my head in towards him. As neither of us were backing down this resulted in both of our foreheads briefly making contact. As our heads touched, I directed our accumulated momentum towards the door. As I was already moving forward I refused to let my head be pushed back. So I just used it to direct him towards the door and outside. Straight after our heads touched he said, 'I'm leaving now, but only cus I want to'. 'Good', I called back. 'Doors right there'.

This whole incident happened in a very short space of time and some of the students looking on had no idea what was happening until our heads touched; they were obviously distracted and not paying attention either. However, immediately after the incident the whole class fell into an awkward stunned silence trying to absorb what had just happened.

At the end of the lesson I once again filled out a referral form and passed it on to my head of department.

A day or so later I then had to have a meeting with the head of department and another senior member of staff to talk about the incident and how I was getting on with this group. It seems gossip had gone around school that I had headbutted the student.

I once again explained the issues I was having with this group and what had happened during the incident, but once again I felt that I was not being supported. If anything I felt that they were having a go at me for the way I put myself across. They suggested I change my ways as I was coming across as aggressive in my nature. I felt this was quite unfair considering the amount of stress and pressure I had been under for the last year or so now.

This was definitely not my nature and it really upset me. As I tried to explain myself to them I was trying not to get too upset but a tear had already began to roll down my cheek. I was absolutely frustrated with the predicament I had found myself in. What upset me the most was deep down I knew that I didn't want to be this person that they thought I was coming across as. It was not my way, and it was not the Sikh way. My parents had not brought me up to be aggressive or be a bully. But I always knew that if I saw vulnerable people being attacked or taken advantage of then I would defend them without a moment of doubt. But it was obvious that to others this was seen as me being aggressive and treating the classroom as a battlefield.

That was not the message I wanted to give out. I wanted to look after people and help them, not hurt them, and that included the student I had the altercation with. I became frustrated with him because I wanted him to achieve and do well.

That evening when I got home I talked to Rav about what had happened at school. As I began telling her I became upset again. She could see I was cracking under the pressure.

I was not a child any more but it still felt the same; not being able to express myself as I wanted to because I was becoming far too upset and my words were not coming out. This time however, I had all the words, but the upset was caused because I kept thinking about my father and how upset he would get when he could not express himself. I told Rav I could see no way out other than to make a clean break as the job was doing irreparable damage to my life – our life. I had to get out to save myself. I could no longer see a future at John Port School. I didn't want this to be my future. I told her I could try something else, like finishing off my driving instructor course, which I had initially began in August 2006 not long after I had completed my NQT year. And if that didn't work out I could still return to teaching somewhere else. The bottom line was that I needed to get out to start afresh.

Most importantly of all though, I needed to mourn for my father properly. To take some time out and reflect what my life had become and what it could still be. Rav agreed. She stood by me and accepted my decision. Knowing full well how it could affect us financially in the long run.

In all honesty, I didn't want the student back in my group, because I knew that things might kick off again and it wouldn't be fair on either of us if it did happen again. But that was not to be. Management decided to let him return to my group.

That was the kind of thing that happened at the school, at the time. I remember on one occasion when a student bit a teacher and once again the student was left in that particular group and not moved out. This was obviously a great annoyance to the teacher who had been bitten, as well as all their colleagues.

As soon as I realised that from now on, this was the way I would be treated in school by the management I gave up writing any more referral forms. There was just no point. Once again I had to deal with things on my own. This incident left a bitter taste in my mouth, not in relation to the heads meeting but how it was handled afterwards.

When the student did return to my group, the very next lesson, we just got on with things and carried on as if nothing had happened. I don't think the incident had any lasting negative effect on our relationship. In the end it really was just a meeting of two minds. Two very stubborn minds who deep down probably had a mutual respect for each other.

The biggest thing I learned from this incident was that children make mistakes and that's OK, I can deal with that. They are still young, they have plenty of time to rectify their behaviour before they become adults. As long as they learn from their mistakes and move on that's perfectly fine. It's ok to make mistakes when you are young. For that reason I always tried to give children the benefit of the doubt, as I knew they could change. Adults on the other hand – if you were going to mess around with me you would be given one chance and that's it. For that reason I always tried my best with the children and never truly gave up on them.

After this incident blew over I once again felt disappointed in myself that my frustrations had got the better of me. I was taking them out on the students whether they deserved it or not. I was snapping at them. I just didn't want to be this person any more. Mr Negative. I wanted to be positive. I was stressing myself out with things beyond my control. Although I could try to influence them in my classroom, it didn't always work out that way. The job was killing me. It was frustrating me beyond belief. One final incident in particular ultimately forced my decision and convinced me for good that it was now time to leave this nest and spread my wings.

One day I was teaching a group of Year 8s when a pigeon flew in through an open window at the back of the lab and then perched itself on the windowsill.

As the pigeon entered the lab many of the students who had heard it flutter in began screeching in panic. The startled pigeon swiftly flew straight back out. 'Calm down', I shouted over their animated chatter. 'Don't be afraid. Us Derby folk love our pigeons'. 'Why Sir? Tell us Sir'. A few of the students called back. I hesitated for a split second; the lesson had already been disrupted. But the students wouldn't stop nattering about what sharp teeth and talons the pigeons had. 'Well if you're going to talk pigeons. I'll give you a pigeon to talk about. Anyone heard of the King of Rome?', I asked. 'No, No' they all excitedly answered back. 'In that case I better tell you a story'. I walked back to my PC at the front of the lab then did an online search for the lyrics of Dave Sudbury's - The King of Rome. 'Ok, listen up. I want no talking as I share this with you'. I grabbed at the lapels of my blazer;

The King of Rome.

In the West End of Derby lives a working man,
He says, 'I can't fly but my pigeons can.
And when I set them free,
It's just like part of me
Gets lifted up on shining wings.'

Charlie Hudson's pigeon loft was down the yard
Of a rented house in Brook Street where life was hard.
But Charlie had a dream,
And in nineteen thirteen
Charlie bred a pigeon that made his dream come true.

There was gonna be a champions' race from Italy.
'Look at the maps, all that land and sea,
Charlie, you'll lose that bird.'
But Charlie never heard,
He put it in a basket and sent it off to Rome.

On the day of the big race a storm blew in,
A thousand birds were swept away and never seen again.
'Charlie, we told you so,
Surely by now you know
When you're living in the West End
there ain't many dreams come true.'

'Yeah, I know, but I had to try,
A man can crawl around or he can learn to fly.
And if you live round here,
The ground seems awful near;
Sometimes I need a lift from victory.'

I was off with my mates for a pint or two
When I saw a wing flash up in the blue.
'Charlie, it's the King of Rome
Come back to his West End home,
Come outside quick, he's perched up on your roof.'

'Come on down, your Majesty, I knew you'd make it back to
me.
Come on down, my lovely one,
You made my dream come true.'

When I had finished reciting the lyrics from memory as well as using the PC as a prompt, there was a continued moment of silence. Then suddenly the whole class erupted into thunderous applause and cheering.

A prickly sense of embarrassment raced through me as I thought, 'what would the other teachers think about all this shouting in my lesson?'. I looked back towards the open window where the pigeon had originally flown in from and then just as quickly flown straight back out, to pastures new. At that moment I also realised that I too had to do the same. My time at John Port School as a teacher of science was nearing its end. This academic year would be my last.

I knew it would be a major gamble to walk away but as Charles Hudson said 'Yeah, I know, but I had to try'. The stray pigeon had made me realise the importance of Derby in my life. My home. Where all of my childhood memories lay. The urge to always want to go home and be with my people no matter where I went or how far I would go. There would always be something pulling me back. Just like the indomitable King of Rome and its desire to return home. Derby.

The King of Rome had put Derby on the map. Somehow I knew that whatever I would do or wherever I would go in life. That same indomitable spirit would also lift me on shining wings. I loved telling stories about all things Derby related with everyone I met. It was now my time to try and give something back to my people and my city.

On that day science didn't fly out the window for me; it became the window. I could now finally see a way out. It was my opportunity to do something that would make me happy; to follow my dreams. I wasn't going to run this time. I was going to walk away with my head held high. I had found a purpose in my life on my way towards my quest for happiness. The answer had revealed itself, blowing in the wind.

Pigeons have always been an ever-present companion in my life and a reminder of home. Their constant cooing from the pear tree in my neighbour's back garden on Portland Street, always gave me a sense of safety and security that soothed my soul.

During my Pear Tree Junior School days we used to watch a wonderful BBC Look and Read educational programme called 'Geordie Racer'. The story was set in Newcastle-upon-Tyne and the surrounding area. It featured pigeon racers and runners competing in the Great North Run. The main character was called Spuggy Hilton (Spuggy being a nickname – the Geordie word for Sparrow). Spuggy was not a runner like the rest of his family, but instead was a keen pigeon fancier and owner of 'Blue Flash' – one of the best birds in Newcastle. The Father of Spuggy was played by the actor Kevin Whately of Auf Wiedersehen, Pet. The theme tune was sung by Derek Griffiths of 'Play School' fame.

At the time of sharing the story of the King of Rome with my John Port School students, I was already well aware of Derby's legendary racing pigeon. However, it was only years later that I found out that a Derby man called Dave Sudbury had written the original lyrics to what is in my opinion the greatest folk song ever. To my astonishment, I found out that Dave Sudbury was also a Normanton boy. Not only that, but he was a Pear Tree boy too. In his youth he had attended the same school as my father, when Pear Tree Junior School was previously called Pear Tree Boys' School. We had all attended the same school building.

Another man who really left his mark on me during my Pear Tree School years and for many years thereafter was a teacher called Steve Wetton. I first met him at Pear Tree Juniors when our class teacher was absent one day; Mr Wetton came in to cover for her.

As my class walked into our classroom that day we noticed Mr Wetton hovering around the back of the room looking up and down at the large wooden framed windows. Once we had all sat down he slid one of the windows open, shivered theatrically and then let out a huge yawn as he stretched out his arms and pumped his fists towards the ceiling. 'What a beautiful gay day'. The whole class looked at him in awe as some also giggled at his choice of words. I also smiled, but I knew exactly what he meant by the word gay, even though many of my classmates may not have. He had introduced a word that many of us only knew in a negative context to tease or ridicule. Having noticed our reaction he then explained, 'gay means happy, didn't you know? There's nothing wrong with being happy. It's ok to say gay. It's ok to be happy'. I smiled, indeed it was.

Mr Wetton only ever taught me for that one day. But during that day he told us all many stories about growing up in the West End of Derby and his subsequent life, how he had written comedy sketches for the Bobby Davro show, in particular the nunchaku skipping rope sketch, how he had once played for Derby County F.C. during his younger days and how he loved to write. He must have been in his late 40s at the time and I remember thinking, 'Wow, he's written for television and he writes plays. He must be the most famous person I have ever met'. I loved his sense of humour and the way he would play with his words and make jokes when he would share his stories.

About ten years later I was working as a cashier in Kwik Save, Littleover during my Mackworth College days when I noticed Mr Wetton making his way to my till with his family. 'Hello Sir' I said. 'Do you know me?' he asked. 'Yes, you taught me once at Pear Tree Junior School'. And then a few years ago I watched the BBC TV programme that you wrote called Growing Pains which starred Ray Brooks and Sharon Duce'. A big smile flashed across his face. I never forgot your stories Sir.

I was very pleased with myself that day that I was able to pluck up the confidence to then strike up a conversation with Mr Wetton, to let him know that I had continued to follow his career. He had always been an inspiration to me and someone I aspired to be like.

The King of Rome had set me free. I would make a clean break. But I had to plan my escape in detail and only engage with trusted colleagues incase the news got out too early. The last thing I wanted was for the students or management to find out before I had even submitted my notice. Operation DynaMo and my evacuation would be carried out on my terms and my terms only.

When I first began at John Port School I had always planned to stay for a five-year cycle, but now I was certain it was only going to be two and this year would be my last. I had itchy feet; I had an urge to go home, to move on. Just like I once had when I was a pupil at Pear Tree Junior School and I so desperately wanted to make the leap up to Village Community School.

Ofsted had made it's decision and I could not see a happy future at this school any longer. I needed to leave it all behind and make a fresh start.

I handed in my notice on Friday, May 25th 2007 and my life instantly changed for the better. A great weight had been lifted from my shoulders and the dark clouds above began to disappear too. I became much more relaxed; the end was near and I could see the light at the end of the tunnel once again.

My self-planned evacuation from John Port School had become my own Dunkirk moment. A personal Operation DynaMo in honour of my father Mohinder Singh.

The actual evacuation of Dunkirk, code-named Operation Dynamo occurred on Sunday, May 26th 1940. It was also known as the Miracle of Dunkirk, which involved the evacuation of Allied soldiers from the beaches and harbour of Dunkirk, France, during World War II.

In this evacuation a flotilla of 700 merchant marine boats, fishing boats, pleasure craft, and lifeboats were called into service for the emergency. These Little Ships of Dunkirk were private boats that sailed from Ramsgate in England to Dunkirk in France between 26th May and 4th June 1940 as part of Operation Dynamo. These little ships helped to rescue more than 338,000 British and French soldiers who were trapped on the beaches at Dunkirk during World War II.

As I had come to terms with the fact that this year would be my last. My relationships with the students immediately began to improve. And I also became a lot more chilled out and relaxed. Over the next couple of months I enjoyed my time at school immensely as I shared more and more stories with them all. Planting seeds and nuggets of information the students would carry with them for the rest of their lives. Life had become fun again.

Although I would still get frustrated though with some groups and their lack of concern for their end of year exams. Especially my lower set Year 11s that I had begun the previous year with. There were still many characters in that class who had given up the ghost a long time ago. My higher set Year 11s on the whole seemed to want to do well though and many of them continued to work hard till the end. My Year 9s had completed their SATs and many of them did very well. I was beginning to wind down.

In the second quarter of 2006 I purchased a copy of Animal Crossing: Wild World on my Nintendo DS Lite handheld game console. For the next few months this little game consumed my whole life as I became lost in a little world I had created called, Punjab. I took the role of my character Mo, named after my father.

The world of Animal Crossing was a simple one in which there were no levels to be beaten or bad guys to overcome. It was just a nice pleasant, cheerful village that you and your character had to maintain. You watered flowers, caught fish and insects, dug up fossils, to present to the museum or sell in the local shop. I also grew trees to collect their fruits then sell them in the local shop and used the money to pay off my mortgages for the houses I lived in and regularly extended.

It was a great distraction for me – to become lost in this little world as I helped Mo look after his village. Another great thing about this game was that three of my Year 8 students also played it. So we would always talk about it in class and share our progress and exchange tips. I once even brought my DS and cheat device into school. I asked these students to bring in their cartridges, which then allowed me to stock up their villages with huge amounts of cash while the three of them were in the process of doing an end of topic test.

All throughout my time at John Port School I loved marking tests to see how well the students had done. I loved returning them, especially to the one's who genuinely tried their best at all times. It was great to see their smiling faces when they saw their scores at the top of the paper. I loved that part of teaching. Seeing the smiles of accomplishment and the distant looks into the ether as they contemplated their future.

Another great thing about that final year was the way Derby County F.C. progressed through the league and eventually would make their way all the way to Wembley in the play offs.

In my final days I made sure to have fun with the students, I had already let them know I was leaving. With one year group I handed out some pictures of SpongeBob SquarePants characters to colour in.

In the previous year I had accidently called a child a pillock. And when he went home and told his mother she called the school. My head of department then asked me if I had called a child a pillock. I said I had, but it was meant in terms of his stupidity and silly behaviour in lessons. However, what I did not realise at the time (and later what a Google search revealed) was that the origins of the word pillock were from the mid-sixteenth century. A variant of archaic pillicock 'penis'. The early sense of pillock in northern English. As soon as I found this out I apologised to the student in question and the next time we had an opportunity to have a fun lesson to celebrate an occasion I printed out some SpongeBob characters for his class to colour in for Christmas. This student shared the same name as Patrick Starfish and he was more than happy to colour it in. It was one of the best lessons I ever had with that class. The joy of silence.

In my final lessons with all my groups I gave many of my students some Dixon Ticonderoga pencils. Roald Dahl had been a big fan of these pencils and I had ordered boxes of them from the US. I also gave away my collection of Doctor Who videos that I had recorded from the TV as a child when I watched them as UK Gold repeats. I gave them all to a young student who was an avid Doctor Who fan, just like I used to be at the same age. I even managed to sell a Gold Rose Doctor Who card for him on eBay for £50. I also patched things up with the student I had the altercation with. On our last lesson together, he had a photo taken with me. I shook his hand and wished him all the best in life. He smiled.

On my final day at school as a Teacher of Science my fellow science teachers presented me with a maillot jaune, Tour de

France yellow jersey. I stood up from my own little space in the corner of the staff room and gave a short speech about why I needed to move on and how much I appreciated their help and guidance over the last two years. They really were my pelaton and I would not have got through my time there without them. My last duty at the school was to go out on a rainy day and carry out bus duty. I went out with my umbrella, and wearing the yellow jersey. I owed those staff in the staffroom a great amount of gratitude. In my darkest days they kept me happy. They made me realise that I wasn't alone.

Earlier in the day I had received a bottle of wine from the headmaster as a leaving present, even though I didn't drink. I had also been asked by an assistant head if I was going to attend the leavers' ceremony at the end of term for the staff that were leaving. I told her I would not, her reaction was to scoff at me then roll her eyes. I didn't care, I had said goodbye to the people that mattered most within the science department and the few scattered across the school that I occasionally met.

Had I stayed any longer at John Port School I would have become absolutely disillusioned and given up completely on teaching. At John Port School I always felt that the NQT program was not making teachers but breaking them, I refused to be broken. The management knew what had happened with my father, well I think they all did, but I can't actually remember the Headmaster ever asking me how I was getting on. The NQT coordinator definitely knew that I had lost my father. Either way I didn't care because I just got on with things to the best of my ability and always had my fellow science teachers for support.

School was finally over, I had to leave, for my own happiness, and I had stuck it out as long as I could. It was the hardest period of my life up to that point. Not only with the loss of my father but having to begin a new career, and I had only recently gotten married too. Life had given me the greatest punch in the stomach, but I had stood firm and not fallen. Nothing could ever come close to these last two years in terms of adversity. I walked away with my head held high. I did my best and I didn't give up.

It was sad to leave. I had never ever planned for it to end like this. I had high hopes of being there for many years and building myself a teaching career, but my time was cut short. On my last day I thought back to the time I had sent an email to the popular science author and mathematician, Simon Singh to let him know that I was to become a Science Teacher. He had replied with some great words of encouragement about how I would change and enrich the lives of all those I would teach and what a great profession it was.

As I drove out of the school gates for the last time, as a member of staff, I thought of the Doctor. The Doctor never lost. Even in apparent death, the Time Lord would regenerate and become anew again. There was always hope to start again. That was one thing I was certain of.

At the end of my time at John Port School on reflection I must admit that when all was said and done and no matter how frustrated and annoyed some of the children made me at times. It is because of them that I survived – in all that time after my father's death, in good and bad situations. They kept me distracted and they kept me busy living. In my case my own personal Operation DynaMo was the deliverance of these hundreds of little shipmates who carried me through to less troubled waters.

*

Around the time I was in the process of completing my last few weeks as a teacher at John Port School. Rav and I were also making plans to move out of our home in Pear Tree. We had been thinking about our long-term future for a while now and hoping to one day start a family of our own.

After a period of house hunting, Rav and I finally chose the house we wanted. I was still reluctant to move away from Pear Tree. I just didn't like change. I say reluctant, but really it was more a case of not wanting to get too involved in these matters, which result in further stress. Rav therefore, did most of the work to secure the new house out and make the initial offers. Having sorted things out with the bank, the mortgage side of things were almost complete, however, Rav was still worried because my decision to finish working at John Port School also coincided with our period of house hunting. So if anything the process of buying a house accelerated and putting an offer in because of my job situation became paramount. We both wanted to make sure that we got the whole house deal completed before my final day as an employee, which was effectively the last day of the 2007 summer holiday. So, what that meant was that I would definitely have to find some type of work again after the summer holidays had finished but more likely to start this new work at the beginning of 2008. It was my hope not only to take a break during the summer holidays but also extend it for the remainder of the 2007 to use that time to sort and plan the rest of my life.

It was a big gamble to take, to walk away from a secure full time job to nothing, but I was confident my teaching qualifications would see me through and find me some supply work as I tested the waters again and sort new teaching pastures.

Another thing that was awaiting me after I left John Port School was a trip to India with Rav, my sister and my mother.

The trip had been planned for some time as my sister was set to get married in April 2008 the following year. This trip would be used for my mother and sister to purchase all the clothing and jewellery they required for the big occasion ahead.

Myself, Rav, my mother and my sister would make this journey together. It would also be my first main break, away from teaching and a chance to return to my parents' homeland of the Punjab. An opportunity for me to make a clean break too. To not have to stress over returning and then going straight back into teaching at John Port School, knowing that I would never go back. I was still anxious over an uncertain future though and the equally uncertain path that life would now take me on.

Just before we all departed for India, Rav and I had to attend a wedding. At the Gurdwara I caught sight of my friend's new grandfather in law, the legendary Sikh distance runner Fauja Singh. It was a great honour to be in the presence of one of my great heroes. So I wasn't going to allow myself to miss the opportunity of talking to him. After a period of hesitation I plucked up the courage to walk over to him and introduce myself. My friend Ather, then took a photograph of Fauja Singh and myself.

A few minutes later I met some old acquaintances of mine from my Pear Tree School days who were now part of the Guru Arjan Dev Gurdwara Football Club in Derby. During our chat I informed them that once I had returned from India, I would be free over the holidays and beyond if they required my assistance. I knew very well that I needed to keep myself busy and distracted on my return. So what better way to do so than begin to engage with my local community whilst also enjoying the beautiful game of football again.

As we waited in the departures lounge I remembered the words my father said to me when I first began applying for NQT positions and had been unsuccessful on the first couple of occasions, 'Don't worry. You will find something. Keep trying'. My father always had faith in me. I wouldn't let him down. I would have to call upon these words after my return from Punjab since I knew full well that I didn't have another job lined up, and I still questioned whether or not I wanted to carry on teaching.

Just before we departed on to the plane to India, a last phone call was made to make sure that the transfer of our deposit for the mortgage had been completed and that the house in the Blagreaves area of Sunny Hill was finally ours.

Once we were all seated comfortably in the plane, I cast my memory back to my Village Community School days and the day Mrs Dancer my English teacher gave us all a hand-out of a Robert Frost poem called 'The Road Not Taken'. After all these years I still had it in my possession at home. It had struck a chord within me as a teenage schoolboy from the moment I first read it. I had never forgotten the underlying message and it still resonated within me after all these years.

On the actual handout itself I had made annotations. Mrs Dancer had asked us to write down some literal and metaphorical notes as to what the poem was about. Now in a literal sense the poem was obviously about walking in a forest. However, in a metaphorical sense the poem was about life in general.

I thought back to the metaphorical notes I had written down.

- 'You can't travel one road and then wonder for the rest of your life. What would have happened if I travelled the other road?'.
- 'You can't always follow the path/road that is well travelled'.
- 'Life is a risk whether to go one way or the other, which may make a big difference'.
- 'No regrets'.
- 'There are knock on effects to decisions'.

On further contemplation another quote from Robert Frost came to mind.

'A poem begins as a lump in the throat, a sense of wrong, a homesickness, a lovesickness'.

My own quest for happiness had begun with a lump in my throat. A sense of wrong after the suicide of my father. A homesickness to want to return home. A lovesickness – to want to love and enjoy life again.

Home was calling.

Chapter 15: Fields of Dreams

School was over, and teaching at John Port School was finally behind me and the house in Littleover was ours. The next journey would be a visit to my parents' homeland.

In the three weeks we were in Punjab, we spent all our time in Sahabpur with my mother's side of the family. The reason we did not stay in Ram Rai Pur was because at the time, work was progressing on a new build. The original home was now no more and a new three-storey house was emerging.

I visited Ram Rai Pur a few times with my mother to visit the site of the old house as well as to meet other family and friends. It was quite sad to see my father's childhood home no longer standing, but it still felt like home as the memories of times gone by and distant voices from the past still resonated within me. The spirit of my father and echoes of yesteryear still remained. The village of Ram Rai Pur had changed considerably over the years. The sons, who had been sent by their families to pastures new around the world, had returned. With their hard work and the savings they sent back, they had built new homes for loved ones who were left behind. On the plot of land where my father's old family home once stood, there were now two new houses that belonged to my family and the family of Sohan Singh Dhindsa, my eldest thiah.

Whilst in Punjab we travelled far and wide to meet my side of the family as well as Rav's. Whilst doing this we also visited many shops where my mother, sister and Rav were able to purchase items for the wedding.

Throughout this whole stay in Punjab the climate was very hot and humid, so I would try not to exert myself too much and become overheated. I would therefore spend much of my time when it was far too hot to do anything, reading a book whilst sitting in the shade next to a big cooling fan. As I slowly flicked through the pages of my book I would also spray water onto my face with a small portable electric hand held fan. The book I had taken along with me on my travels was called 'Shoeless Joe' by W.P. Kinsella.

The book is much better known due to it's film adaptation; 'Field of Dreams' which starred Kevin Costner, Amy Madigan, James Earl Jones, Ray Liotta and Burt Lancaster, in his final role.

The protagonist Ray Kinsella and the link to his father were at the heart of the story. I had been a huge fan of the film and the story itself mesmerised me. Whilst reading the book I would regularly have to take breaks away from it as images and thoughts in relation to the story began to consume my mind. The myriad of fields and great expanses of green all around me added to the sensation of also walking in Ray Kinsella's footsteps. It additionally left within me a feeling of wanting to follow in Ray Kinsella's footsteps too when I returned home to Derby. The walking, the reading and the overwhelming contemplation had awakened my dreams.

The more I read of 'Shoeless Joe' the more I was compelled to want to return to Derby and do something with my life. I wanted to build something. I wanted to leave something behind after my death. At the time I did not know exactly what, but deep down the same message from the book had also left it's mark within me. The Voice: 'If you build it he will come. Ease his pain. Go the distance'.

I stretched out the reading of 'Shoeless Joe' for as long as I could. It was not because it was a bad read. But because it was such a brilliant story and I didn't want it to end. The downside to finishing the book was that once this mesmerising distraction had been taken away from me I then began to think more and more about returning home, to Derby, and eventually having to find another job.

One year previously, I had spent the summer holidays visiting Scotland with Rav, but at no point on the trip was I able to switch off completely from thinking about the looming new academic year ahead. All those people who think that teachers have it easy with their six-week summer holidays have no idea about the stress and anxieties we all go through during that period. The planning and preparation that we have to put into our work before a new academic year even begins can be quite punishing on many of us. Thankfully, it was a great relief knowing that when I returned from Punjab I wouldn't go straight back into teaching. Although, my anxieties about finding another job did make me reflect on my teenage years and my first tentative steps into employment.

When I left Village Community School in 1996 my father decided that it would be a good idea for me to get a job during the summer holidays before I enrolled at Mackworth College. This was so that I could earn some money whilst also gaining some valuable work experience. My father and my masser, Darbara thus found myself and my cousin, Satnam, a job. This particular job was on a farm in Sinfin, which was managed by a supposed friend of my father and masser.

Satnam and I were there for two days picking pea pods from the vine fields and the work was absolutely backbreaking. After our first day we really didn't want to go back the next morning, but my father managed to change our minds. We were still unhappy from the previous day too when we had been paid for one day's work in cash. Even though we both did the same work I was paid less because I was younger, and we both felt we did not get paid enough anyway.

The next morning we were full of cramp but still managed to get on with the work. However as the hours went by Satnam and I decided that we'd had enough. Some of the old men that we had been working with had been doing our heads in and were not very nice or polite to us either. So during a little break we both hatched a plan of escape. At one point we stood up and walked a short distance away from the main group of workers. When we noticed that we were not being watched we then ran as fast as we could away from them all whilst laughing our heads off at the silliness of our predicament. As we weaved in and out through the fields of vegetation, we occasionally looked back through the gaps between the vines to make sure that the angry old men were not in pursuit. After a short period of intense running we finally reached the safety of the other side of the large field and then quickly ran into a red telephone box. Once inside Satnam pulled some change out of his pocket and made a call to our friend Suntokh. He could now drive and had his own car. Satnam began explaining to him about the predicament we had found ourselves in, where we were and how we needed to get back home to Pear Tree, before we were caught and possibly frog marched into the pea fields again.

Pear Tree was not too far from Sinfin so we knew that Suntokh wouldn't take too long to drive from his home on Harrington Street to Sinfin. As we waited for him under a bridge, Satnam and I began skimming stones into the canal. After a few minutes we noticed a vehicle approaching, so we leaped out from under the bridge to try and get Suntokh's attention. However, as the vehicle approached we immediately saw the colourful bright orange turban of the driver and realised it was not Suntokh but our fathers' supposed friend we were supposed to be working for. As soon as we realised we had been flagging down the wrong man we both quickly legged it back under the bridge and fell into a heap on the floor in absolute hysterics.

Suntokh finally arrived a few minutes later and was able to take us both away from our painfully amusing nightmare. Our fathers' were not very pleased with us that day because we had done a runner. But I think deep down they were happy that Satnam and I had both learned a valuable lesson; stay in school, get yourself an education and then you will never have to work in places like that again. Our fathers might have been accustomed to working like that in the old days but from that day on I knew there was no way I wanted to do anything like that again. Although, a couple of years later I did have to do similar work to make a bit of money prior to and during my university years, but once again that was another life and work experience.

My father also managed to get me my first proper job at Kwik Save, Littleover. My initial interview didn't go very well as I was a bit naïve at the time and told the store manager that I would be uncomfortable dealing with money. As my father knew the store manager's father I was given a second chance having learnt from my previous mistake and got the job the second time around.

I had some unforgettable moments during my time at Kwik Save working as a cashier on the tills. I worked there during my Mackworth College years four days a week, including weekends. A few incidents still have me rolling around in stitches now as I think back to them and one incident in particular made me feel very let down at the time.

On one occasion a man and his wife came over to my till and asked me where the Bovril was. So I pointed in the direction it was in and off they went to collect it from the shelf on the aisle. A few minutes later they came back to me and said, 'It's not there?'. I looked at the man; 'It's right in front of you, over there'. But just as I began to point it out to them both, I realised that I must have misheard them. 'Hold on, you did say bog roll, right?', I asked awkwardly. 'No, I said Bovril', said the man. At this point we all began laughing and I couldn't suppress my chuckles for the rest of the shift.

On another occasion I was put in charge of the alcohol and tobacco section. I used to love it in there. It was like a big game to me. I didn't smoke, so I had no idea about any of the cigarette brands and my knowledge of the various types of alcohol brands was also quite limited. I obviously picked up the different names and brands as time went on, but to begin with I required help from the customers to point them out to me.

One day a man came in asking for a particular brand of tobacco. As I had no idea where the tobacco was behind me, I politely asked him if he could point it out. I was a bit taken aback when he replied 'No'. The dark glasses and the walking stick should have given me a clue but I totally missed the tell tale signs. 'I'm blind', he then said. I eventually found the tobacco he was looking for and handed it over to him quite apologetically. It could only happen to me and reminded me of the time I bumped into a blind man in town and then awkwardly and apologetically told him, 'Sorry, I didn't see you'.

Another incident involving the alcohol and tobacco section was when I was working in there alone and I decided there was no need for both of the scanners to be on at the same time. So I tried to switch one of them off in the hope of saving some electricity. I had seen two buttons underneath a scanner so I began jabbing at these buttons with two fingers, but nothing seemed to be happening. So I pressed them again and again and still the scanner did not switch off. A couple of minutes later, I began to think, 'hold on a second, what if they were not the on/off switch, but a panic button?'. A minute or so later two out of breath Police Officers came rushing into the store and then began asking me what had happened. I couldn't stop myself from chuckling at the slapstick of it all, as I then had to tell them and the store manager that it was a false alarm and I thought I was switching off the scanners. Fortunately, I didn't get into trouble for it as nobody had alerted me to what the buttons were actually for. I obviously apologised to the Police for wasting their time too.

One final incident really had a lasting effect on my overall character for the rest of my life. A Sikh girl with a turban once came in and bought a Mars bar. She then gave me £30 to pay for it and asked for the change back in pound coins. Now this was not a common occurrence and I guess that is what confused me when I gave the change back to her. I was supposed to give her back one bag of 20 pound coins and some extra change. But I accidently gave her two bags of 20 pound coins and the remaining change. I had wrongly assumed that one bag only contained 10 pound coins. So I inadvertently gave her an extra £20 in change. When I handed all the change back to her I noticed that she did look at me quite puzzled for a brief moment as she then left. A couple of minutes later the mistake dawned on me. My first reaction was to call my father and ask him to bring me a £20 pound note so that I could put it back in the till, as I knew the till would be short. In the end I decided against it and when my till was counted up at the end of the shift I explained that there might be a discrepancy. It was my mistake and I owned up to it. Once again, I didn't get into trouble for it. I was not even docked any wages. However, I felt really let down at the time that somebody could knowingly do this to me and potentially have gotten me in a lot of trouble.

I never forgot that incident, because from that day on I always knew how it felt to make a genuine mistake and then be taken of advantage of because of it. It wasn't a nice feeling to have experienced nor did I ever want to put others in a similar situation whereby I could have taken advantage of them and got them in trouble for my own personal gain. In subsequent years, when similar things have happened to me, and people or cashiers have made mistakes with change, I've always made sure to let them know that they have given me too much change and I have always returned it back on the spot. I also do this when people drop money on the floor without noticing. I pick it up and give it right back to them whatever the amount.

It's called empathy, the ability to understand and share the feelings of another. I first came across the word empathy at Village Community School. I'd picked it up from reading Philip K. Dick's 'Do Androids Dream of Electric Sheep' (Blade Runner) and Isaac Asimov's 'I Robot'. I'd read both books in Mrs Dancer's English Literature classes in the process of writing an essay about the subject of robots and feelings.

After that incident I always tried to play things honestly. Years later, I met the girl again. I didn't say anything. There was no need to. She taught me a valuable lesson in life and I'll always be thankful to her for it.

In the final days of our trip to Punjab we used the time left to say farewell to our family and friends. In the process, I once again decided to hand out some Dixon Ticonderoga pencils to the children.

Throughout our stay in Sahabpur I spent much of my time with my mother's elderly father, Munsha Singh Thiara. My nana had been having issues with his memory for a long while now and clearly showed signs of dementia. His memory would come and go. He would remember the old days but regularly forget about more recent times. I would try to talk to him as much as I could. On some days he seemed to be aware of my father's passing and on other days he would talk about my father as if he was still alive. I found it quite upsetting, that dementia could do this to people and that the memories of times gone by could so easily be lost forever.

On my final day in Punjab I went over to him to say my last goodbye. He was sat in the barn area alone. Deep down I knew it would probably be the last time we would ever speak to each other. I crouched down beside him. In a moment of lucidity he then asked in Punjabi. 'What happened to Mindy?', then he shook his head. I shook my head too as the tears began to fill my eyes. I didn't have the words to explain.

My mother had already said her goodbye to her father and had returned to the awaiting van where Rav and my sister were also waiting for me. It was time to say goodbye. I began to get a bit overcome with emotion as I spoke to him in English, knowing full well he would not understand a word I said. 'Take care nana. When you see Dad, tell him we're all well. Everything will be ok. It's all going to be ok'. With a glint in his eye my nana looked straight back at me and smiled. I gave him one last hug and then began walking back towards the van. As I did so I closed my eyes to contain my tears and then took a long deep breath inhaling through my nose. In that moment my mind stirred up all the great memories of times gone by.

As I set foot into the van, I wiped my tears and looked back at my nana in his barn for the last time. Gandalf the White came to mind and I raised my hand to him. We then passed Gian Singh's family home and made our way out of Sahabpur and towards Amritsar.

On the journey back to England on the plane I had an overwhelming eagerness to get home. W.P. Kinsella's magical story would come back with me to England, although the book itself would be left behind on the plane by Rav. It didn't matter though. 'Shoeless Joe' had planted a seed within me. I could always buy another book and I would have loved it if someone else got to read it and be equally inspired to do something worthwhile with their life. As I drifted in and out of sleep, the same thought kept coming back into my mind. 'If you build it. He will come'. I had no idea who 'He' was. But I knew I was onto something. I'd felt it in my bones.

On our return to Pear Tree I knew that the break had done me some real good. I also knew that I needed to change my ways and pursue happiness no matter what. Surprisingly, there was another thing I was also looking forward to: returning to John Port School again to find out how my ex students had done in their exams.

I was well aware that after I came back from my trip to the Punjab, GCSE results day would also be awaiting. I also knew that it would be the perfect icing on the cake in terms of how I finished at the school.

It was great to go back and see how the students had got on. They all deserved everything they got, whether that be good or bad. On the whole though, I was very proud. For the first time in my adult life I felt that I had actually done something worthwhile to help others achieve. I had made a difference and done some real good for my people. I was especially overjoyed with my higher set science group. I had been their teacher for two years and had tried my utmost to prepare them with everything they needed to succeed. Even though I was having immense difficulties in my personal life I didn't give up on them. Through the gathering storm I had left not one of them behind. Every single student in my Year 11 group passed with an A*-C. In true Shackletonion spirit, by endurance we had indeed conquered. It would act as a great spur for my next mission in life.

Immediately after the euphoria of the GCSE results had passed my feelings of anxiety strangely returned and I began to feel stressed once again. Could the thought of a fast-approaching new academic year have gotten under my skin? Even though I knew full well that once Wednesday, September 5th finally passed I knew I would not be returning to work. Maybe it was the realisation that Rav and I now finally owned our own house that was beginning to stress me out: the thought that I would eventually have to move all my possessions across whilst trying not to lose anything during the transfer. Little things like this rested heavily on my mind.

We decided not to move into the new house until just before my sister's wedding. So after arriving back from Punjab Rav and I continued to live in Pear Tree whilst making regular visits to the new house to make home improvements as well as keep an eye on the builders.

One thing that really did alleviate my worries about finding a job so soon after I returned from Punjab was that I knew that I would still be getting paid by John Port School until the end of the holidays. For this reason I was a lot more relaxed about my financial situation. I was also confident in myself that I could find a new job no matter how much my anxieties told me otherwise. I had to believe that I had my qualifications and, most importantly, I had choices.

Towards the end of my father's life he seemed to accept that working in a bakery was the only job left for him. He could have applied for other jobs but his confidence and self-esteem was always lacking. I think his difficulty in communicating in English always held him back. He felt he had no choices. He felt that he could not better himself. In the end it may have been that he felt that his choices in life just ran out. He still had so much to offer but he just couldn't see the light through his darkness.

A few weeks after we all returned from home, my mother received a phone call from Punjab. My nana, Munsha Singh

Thiara had not been well for a few days and during the previous night the old man of Sahabpur had passed away. I was very saddened by his death but grateful that I was able to meet him one last time before he passed.

On my return to England I carried on reading fervently, book after book. As I now had so much time on my hands, for the first time in a very long time I was able to walk into Derby town centre and visit the Waterstones bookshop.

My reading would follow trends and I would get through a few books at a time in quick succession. The main thread at this moment in my life was obviously Derby. So I began reading as much as I could about the city of Derby. Many of these books were compiled by the likes of Anton Rippon, his daughter, Nicola and others such as Maxwell Craven. Derby was the city in which I was born, and the town where my father first chose to settle with his family. By attaching my father's memory to Derby and vice versa I knew I would never forget him. It was therefore the thing I most associated with my father and the one thing I had to keep hold of and close to my heart.

One day I walked into my bedroom to return the last book I had been reading back onto my bookshelf. As I carefully placed it back into the gap I had created when I pulled it out, I glanced over my bookshelf to make a mental note of all the books I had read in the last couple of weeks. On the second shelf I caught sight of a familiar name. A book that I'd bought a few months previously and had still not got around to reading. I'd been saving it until I felt the time was right. My eyes were now drawn towards it. I instinctively reached out for it and touched the tip of its spine with my left index finger. I then pulled it out, letting it glide out of its position. A ghostly pale face caught my eye and didn't break his stare. A spark of electricity rippled through me as I looked down at the front cover:

Steve Bloomer
The Story of Football's First Superstar
Peter Seddon

It was time.

Chapter 16: Destroying Angel

As soon as I sat down to read the foreword to the book by Steve Richards (Steve Bloomer's grandson) I had become absolutely entranced. The Introduction by the author Peter Seddon captivated me even further.

Upon reading the chapter 'A Derby Lad 1879 – 1886', I came across a passage which truly hit home. Steve Bloomer was a Derby boy just like myself. Although he was born on Tuesday, January 20th 1874 in Cradley, Worcestershire; in 1879 his parents Caleb and Mehrab moved their whole family to Litchurch, Derby.

The superstar I had first stumbled across when I was a child almost 20 years previously was now firmly back in my thoughts. Even more so, when I then set eyes upon another amazing revelation. Steve Bloomer, his wife Sarah and their children used to live in a modest terrace house at 35 Portland Street. This house was a short walk up the road from my own home on 160 Portland Street. This shared connection between us instantaneously filled me with an absolute overwhelming sense of pride. Steve Bloomer was a Pear Tree man just like myself.

Although many of the events in Peter Seddon's Steve Bloomer biography took place a hundred years before I was even born, I recognised every street and place in that book because I had also lived there. As I continued to read, memories of my own past began to flood back to me. More than anything I began to realise that just like Bloomer, my father before me would have also walked down and played on those same streets.

From that moment on all I wanted to do was find out as much as I could about Steve Bloomer and my old neighbourhood of Pear Tree and in the process share these stories with everyone I met. I wanted to spread the legend. I wanted everyone to know that, yes, I am from Derby and yes, I do live in Pear Tree and yes, I will forever be proud. I wanted the world to know about one of the greatest players the game has ever produced: Steve Bloomer: A Pear Tree boy.

Deep down, though, I wanted to connect this pride with the memory of my father. I wanted my father to know that I was proud of him and the area we were all raised within. The last thing I ever wanted to do from now on was reject who I was and where I came from. I knew very well that to reject my community would be to reject my father and to do that would be to forget my father. It would never happen – not in my book. I wanted to be positive again. The last two years of my life had almost knocked all the stuffing out of me. I didn't want to experience any of that negativity ever again.

Peter Seddon's biography of Steve Bloomer had literally given me a new lease of life. Having read the book in its entirety within three days. I was absolutely sure that it would somehow play a significant role in my life thereafter.

Reading about the life of Steve Bloomer had consumed my own existence from that point onwards. It had kept me distracted and taken me back to the good old days where I was at my happiest. But I also knew that I had to try and find other ways to keep myself preoccupied and distracted too. I had to make sure I kept myself busy to not allow my mind to stop for a second. I had to keep my mind ticking over. I had to remain positive and continue to share my enthusiasm.

The next day I decided to leave my house and take a short walk towards Pear Tree library. As I walked up Portland Street I passed my old Harrington Street Nursery on the left and then the Pear Tree Schools on the right. A little further on I passed the Wallis clothing factory on the left then crossed over St Thomas Road and back onto Portland Street. As I stood behind the Jolly Fagman Newsagent I looked over at the house behind the chemist. Steve Bloomer's old home on 35 Portland Street was still standing there after all these years. I stood there for a good few seconds thinking about the people who had once lived there. The times I had passed it myself without knowing its history. I looked towards my left at the old Carnegie Library, the place where I had first glimpsed the face of the legendary Steve Bloomer. I looked to my right and back down Portland Street where I continued to still live. This was my home. These were my people.

Later in the evening I decided to write a review for the book.

Amazon Review by K. S. Dhindsa
Monday, August 20th 2007

'Steve Bloomer – The Story of Football's First Superstar' by Peter Seddon

'For many years now I have known about the legend of Steve Bloomer. When I was younger I used to walk past the main entrance of the Baseball Ground and read the plaque that used to commemorate his exploits. It is only after reading

*this book that I discovered that he used to attend a school down the road from me (Pear Tree School, corner of Pear Tree Street and Portland Street/clothing factory now) and amazingly he used to live on the same street as me. This book is a must read for all Derby's citizens that were born in the city and support Derby County F.C. I have even found myself walking up and down some streets looking out for numbers of old houses he and his family used to live in. It is a great read, even better for the fact that the places that are referred to, time and time again are actual places in Derby that many people who live in the city will recognize. One of the greatest footballers that ever lived and he lived on my street. *smiles* Legend'.*

Wednesday, September 5th 2007 finally arrived. I wasn't in school and I wouldn't be teaching at John Port School. I was free. It was time to get my life in order. But what was I going to do now? Whatever it was, I needed to remain positive and upbeat, as I knew it would be the perfect time for the black dog to awake within me again if I remained idle and unemployed.

In my last few months at John Port School I had realised that the things that made me feel most joy and happiness were the things that made me feel proud. Therefore, it was only right that I should immerse myself in things that filled me with pride. I needed to reclaim all that I had lost to make myself happy again and in the process keep the memory of my father alive.

I was therefore once again drawn back to the message in my father's obituary, which was published in the *Derby Evening Telegraph.*

'NEVER REJECT YOUR OWN COMMUNITY NO MATTER WHAT FAULTS YOU FIND WITHIN IT.'

Reaffirming to myself that I should be proud of who I was and where I came from. Proud to be from Derby. Proud to support Derby County F.C. Proud to be a British born Punjabi Sikh. Proud to be a Doctor Who loving Sikh Derby boy. There would be no more holding back. I would wear my heart on my sleeve. I am a Derby man.

The beginning of October is when I really turned the corner in relation to my life becoming more open and optimistic. Mark Zuckerberg had a massive part to play in this.

By October 2007 Facebook had already been around for just under four years. Membership was initially restricted to the students of Harvard College; within the first month, more than half the undergraduates at Harvard were registered on the service. In March 2004, Facebook expanded to the universities of Columbia, Stanford, and Yale. It later opened to all Ivy League colleges, Boston University, New York University, MIT, and gradually most universities in the United States and Canada. Eventually on Tuesday, September 26th 2006, Facebook was opened to everyone who was 13 years of age or older and with a valid email address.

On Tuesday, October 2nd 2007 I finally decided that the time was right to join Facebook. During the first year of its universal availability I had made sure to avoid it like the plague. At the time, the last thing I wanted was for people to find out who I was and what had happened to my father. In the previous couple of years I was quite used to being a private person who fiercely protected and guarded my privacy. As soon as I signed up, Facebook began to change my life for the better. On Wednesday, October 3rd 2007 I posted and shared my first ever status. It was only right that it was a poem by Robert Frost called 'The Road Not Taken'. On the previous day I had also tried to add my first ever

Facebook friend. With so many names I could have chosen to search for, one name quickly sprang to mind. I had only ever seen him on the TV and I had always wanted to know what became of him, as well as let him know that I had never forgotten him. His name was Satbir Gupta and he was a 'Countdown Champion' for a week in August 1996. At the time of viewing his appearances on Channel 4 he was probably the most famous Sikh I had ever seen on TV. I made sure to watch all his appearances with my father during the week or so that he reigned victorious. The next day he accepted my friend request and we have remained Facebook friends ever since.

Over the next few days I began adding to my friends lists, making contact with long lost people from the past. As I made these links, many memories of my father were also beginning to become alive once again in my imagination. As the days went on I became more and more positive and upbeat. Every day I would wake up and jump out of my bed and straight onto my PC without fail. In the process I was beginning to create memories. Pleasant memories that made me feel good. In time I eventually set up many groups, but one of the first I ever made was 'Homelands Grammar School (Village Community School) Derby'.

One downside to these intense periods on the Internet was that I then spent too much time at home. Although the social interacting was great because of the things I was beginning to find out about the city of my birth. It would then result in feelings of claustrophobia as well as opposite feelings of flight, because I needed to get out of the house to explore and observe. Although I was deliberately keeping myself busy to stop myself from thinking bad thoughts. The isolation at home was also having a negative effect on me. Therefore, I needed to snap out and get out.

Thankfully the perfect opportunity to leave my house arose when I found out that a selection of former Derby County stars would feature in a charity match at the Moorways Bowl on Sunday, October 14th. The event had come up at the perfect time for me. Especially considering that Kevin Hector would be one of the most famous 'All-Stars' on show.

Kevin Hector had scored 268 goals from 662 appearances in the English Football League playing for Bradford Park Avenue and Derby County F.C. At Derby County he made a record 589 appearances during his two spells, 486 of which came in the league and then became a club record. As a goal scorer he scored a total of 201 goals compared to Steve Bloomer's 332. Kevin Hector was also capped twice for England.

If any player could ever match Steve Bloomer's accomplishments at Derby County F.C. then Kevin Hector would always come a very close second. He was up there with the best of them all. For this reason I was adamant that I would go down and meet him. Hoping that I could get close enough to ask him for his autograph.

On the day of the charity match I went down with Rav. I wasn't going to let this opportunity pass me by. Rav knew how much it meant for me to get Kevin Hector's autograph. I had come prepared with my camera, a pen and a book called 'The Who's Who of Derby County' by Gerald Mortimer. It was my hope that Kevin Hector would sign his autograph on the page that his profile was printed on.

The game between the 'Rams All-Stars' and Shelton Sports F.C. kicked off at 2pm. And as Rav and I watched on I noticed some familiar faces from the past on the football pitch. I didn't recognise them all but the players that were in the frame for a place in the 'All Stars' starting eleven were

Neil Bailey, Paul Blades, Steve Crocker, John Davidson, Roger Davies, Andy Garner, Phil Gee, Graham Harbey, Trevor Hebbard, Kevin Hector, Tommy Johnson, Jason Kavanagh, Gary Mills, David Nish, Dick Pratley, Craig Ramage, Steve Taylor and Paul Williams.

As Rav and I continued to watch on from the covered spectator seating I noticed that Kevin Hector was not amongst the players on the pitch nor on the bench along the sidelines. I became a little despondent at noticing this. I did see Roger Davies on the bench though, talking to a few of the substitutes, which lifted my spirits slightly. A few minutes before the half time whistle was about to blow a gentle roar of approval followed by clapping began to resonate from the stands behind me. I looked on open mouthed. A man had been let through the gate in the fence, by a female guard. This elderly man began walking towards the bench in his flared denim jeans and black walking boots. Carrying his rain jacket in his right hand he walked past the sand pit and then joined up with the other players on the bench. As he sat down and talked to the other substitutes he then began to put on his jacket over his blue t-shirt. 'Who's that?' asked Rav. 'It can't be? It's the King' I replied back in disbelief. 'Who?', asked Rav. 'It's Kevin Hector'. I could not believe it.

'I've got to meet him', I said to Rav. 'Go on then. Go ask that lady at the gate' replied Rav. She was right. The only way I would be able to meet Kevin Hector was if the lady at the gate let me through. So I passed my camera onto Rav having already taken some photos and video footage of Kevin Hector walking onto the pitch. I then began to make my way down to the gate. I was nervous and apprehensive. I had every right to be. I was going to ask the lady at the gate if she could let me through so I could ask Kevin Hector for his autograph. As I got to the bottom of the spectators stand I went over to the lady and showed her my book and pen. 'Could you please allow me through the gate so I can ask Kevin Hector for his autograph?', I asked. She was very nice and polite to me but told me that she could not let me through because if she did she would then have to let everyone through. I tried again but to no avail. She then told me that at the end of the game all the players would meet up in the Golden Pheasant pub and I could try to get his autograph there. I then had to explain to her that I didn't drink and would not be able to make it down there. I looked back at Rav in the stands and shook my head at her whilst gesticulating apparent defeat. I didn't return to my seat though and I carried on talking to the lady at the gate. I began telling her how much I wanted to see Kevin Hector because I had never met him before and how my late father who was not the biggest football fan was still aware of him and would tell me how good a player Kevin Hector was. I also told her about the time Roy McFarland had walked past me at the train station and I was unable to get his autograph either. A couple of minutes later the half time whistle went and I was still standing at the gate. The lady then told me that she needed to go for a toilet break. Just before she went off she made sure to tell me that at no point should I open the gate to make my own way towards the pitch. A few minutes later she returned and noticed that I was still standing where she had last seen me. 'I didn't go, I told you I wouldn't', I said. The last thing I wanted was for her to get into trouble due to a perceived selfish act on my behalf. So I stood my ground and waited till she got back. Having seen that I wasn't a troublemaker and genuinely only wanted to meet Kevin Hector she then surprised me by opening the gate. 'Go on, off you go. Come back quickly though', she said. I couldn't believe it. 'You sure?', I asked. 'Yes, hurry up before I change my mind', she smiled. My tenacity had paid off.

As I approached the wooden bench the first person I bumped into was Roger Davies. I shook his hand and said hello then quickly explained to him what I was up to. He then took my book off me and signed his autograph next to his profile and picture. 'Who else have you bookmarked here?', he then asked. 'Kevin Hector', I replied. Roger then raised his hand and then pointed in the direction of Kevin Hector who was sitting only two places to the left of him. Kevin then looked back towards the stands possibly wondering how many more people might join me. Nobody else did though. I walked over to Kevin Hector, shook his hand then I offered him my book. Kevin held my book then began flicking through the pages as he found his own profile page. I then offered him my pen. As he signed his autograph next to his picture I said to him 'It's an honour to meet you'. I had waited 20 years for that autograph. It wasn't Bloomer's, but it was the next best thing. Kevin Hector was the only man who ever came remotely close to Steve Bloomer's Derby County F.C. records.

I refused to walk away that day until I got his autograph. I was relentless and in the end the lady at the gate yielded to my requests because she knew she could trust me. Kevin Hector didn't play that day, but I did see him march onto the pitch. He was 62 years old at the time. Two years younger than Steve Bloomer was when he died.

*

A month or so previously I had made contact with the coaching staff at the Guru Arjan Dev Gurdwara Football Club. During one weekend I hooked up with the Under 12s who were coached by Minder Singh Shanan. We'd travelled down to the Racecourse Playing Fields for a match. Just before kick off I told the boys about the history of the old Racecourse Ground and how it was once Derby County F.C.'s home before they moved to the Baseball Ground. I also told them about how a legendary footballer by the name of Steve Bloomer once played on this turf too. When training was over, I dropped a few of the boys at their homes in Normanton and as I did so I pointed out some of the houses that Steve Bloomer had once lived with his family. Having never heard of who Steve Bloomer was before this day, they now knew that he was a Pear Tree legend, but did everyone else?

Chapter 17: Good Old Derby

I was still on a great high after meeting Kevin Hector and Roger Davies the day before, so I decided to spend the rest of the following week walking around the streets of Pear Tree and Normanton retracing the footsteps of Steve Bloomer.

As I was reading through Peter Seddon's biography I had bookmarked numerous pages within the book with scraps of paper. These bookmarks were in relation to some of the homes that Steve Bloomer had once inhabited or other places of interest that were relevant to his life in Normanton. When I had finished reading the book I created a list of all these places that I would then visit at a later date.

On Monday, October 15th I visited the following places on my list and made sure to take a photo at each location.

Steve Bloomer: The Story of Football's First Superstar

Pear Tree School

'As a 5 year old Stephen Bloomer went to Pear Tree School, then just a tiny Church of England Mission School on the

corner of Pear Tree Street and Portland Street, still there today, but now the premises of a clothing manufacturer.'

102 St Thomas Road (Shield)

'On the same day, Phillip's under-15 side won the Junior School Shield, not a bad day's work for the Bloomer boys. Even to this day a reminder of the prestige attached to the shield can be seen close to the site of the Vulcan Ground on a replica built into the brickwork of a house at 102, St Thomas's Road, placed there by the proud building contractor John Chapman, whose own team Wellingborough Villa once took the trophy.'

41 St Thomas Road

'Against such a backdrop the Bloomers moved on from Yates Street, possibly prompted by the death of their lodger Joseph Harlow or Steve's newly enhanced earnings. By the start of 1896 Caleb and family had moved into a more recently built terraced house at 41 St Thomas's Road, still there today and now an electrical shop. Close to Ley's works and the football ground, it suited Caleb and the two oldest Bloomer lads perfectly.'

91 Dairy House Road

On 27 May 1902 the 'sugar and spice' hat trick was complete, Doris Alexandra being born at Cummings Street. That seems to have prompted a move up-market from the 3-bedroom terrace to a 4-bedroom house at 91 Dairy House Road, just a street away from the Baseball Ground and recently built on the fields where Steve might once have shot at sticks. Again the house was marginally one of the best in the road, an end-of-terrace this time with a small foregarden and adjacent the church.'

35 Portland Street

'He moved into 35 Portland Street, quite a substantial end-terrace house with a small foregarden right on his home patch, no more than a short walk from all his previous boyhood and marital homes and just a 5 minute stroll from the Baseball Ground (1910–1936)'

St Thomas's Church

'Stephen Bloomer and Sarah Walker were married on a Wednesday afternoon, 19 August 1896, at St Thomas's Church.'

44 Yates Street

'Judged against such a backdrop, the Bloomers were a modern and progressive family for their time and Caleb deserves full credit for having the initiative to make the move. Their first home was a rented terraced house at 44 Yates Street, now demolished but then just off Pear Tree Road on the fringe of New Normanton, only a few minutes walk from the open fields which were later to become the Baseball Ground.'

87 Yates Street

'The Bloomer family had continued to grow during Stephen's schooldays by the addition of 'one of each' – Emma in 1882 and David in 1884. As a result of that expansion, Caleb and Merab, still only in their 30's at the time of David's birth, had moved over the road with their 5 children to 87 Yates Street.'

St James Road Infant School

'The school Stephen actually attended between the ages of 6 and 12, from 1880 to 1886, and for which Caleb might well have had to pay a small weekly fee known as "school pence", was the newly-constructed St James's Road Board School,

specially erected to cater for the huge influx of youngsters into the area and designed to take 1,500 pupils at full capacity. Situated and (still) standing, but under a different name, towards the bottom of St James's Road on land bounded by Hastings Street and Wright Street (Now Dover Street) it was just a few hundred yards from his Yates Street home.'

No longer standing.

81 Cummings Street

'Their first child, Hetty Winifred, was born at Cummings Street 18 months into the marriage on 15th February 1898; with a second child later on the way the young family moved over the road in preparation, to number 81, a terraced house extending over the entry with an extra bedroom, and on 30th April 1900 another girl duly arrived. (Violet Pretoria).'

34 Cummings Street

'Just 22 and 21, Steve and Sarah (Bloomer) set up home at 34 Cummings Street off Normanton Road, a typical terraced sized house still standing trim and neat now, the only one in the street structurally detached, perhaps just a hint of one-

upmanship which reflected Steve's earning power and Sarah's preference.'

There were also two other places on my list in Derby, which I didn't visit on the day, but I knew I would visit very soon. The Great Northern Inn Pub on 19 Junction Street, Derby and Nottingham Road Cemetery.

The third and final place that was on my list was 34 Parliament Street in Middlesbrough and I would make sure to visit it the next time I would go up north with Rav to see her parents.

As I walked around the streets of Normanton with my camera and list in the process of tracing the footsteps of Steve Bloomer, I began to remember the times that I had passed these same places and buildings with my own father. I was literally tracing not only my own steps but my father's too.

My visit to Cummings Street had been one of the best surprises of all as directly outside number 34 would have been the exact spot my father would have parked his car when we would regularly visit my eldest masser, Karnail

Singh Rai and his family who used to live at number 41 across the road.

Normanton had changed a lot since the days of my youth. It was no longer what it used to be. And to think, even before then it would no doubt have been in a much better state during Steve Bloomer's days. How times had changed.

My form once had a lesson in the Pear Tree Building at Village Community School with a jolly giant of a teacher called Mr Golding. During this lesson we were asked to rate the neighbourhood in which we lived. Paying particular attention to the condition of the roads, the pavements, the trees, whether there was any litter and the overall attractiveness of the area. After a few minutes we were all told to put our pencils down and then prepare to share our scores, out of ten with the rest of the class.

My hand shot up immediately with pencil in hand, the eraser jabbing towards the ceiling. 'Go on then Kal, what's your score?', asked Mr Golding. 'Ten Sir', I replied with my hand still jabbing in the air. 'And where exactly do you live, Kal? 'Portland Street, Pear Tree, Sir', I promptly replied. The whole class erupted into laughter. 'That's a dump', I heard someone call out through the laughter from behind me. A little grimace flashed across my face after a moment's deflation. My hand began to fall. As I brought it down towards my piece of paper I swiveled my pencil around and rubbed away at the number 1. I then turned the 0 into a 9. A dump it may have been to them, but to me ... I was proud of where I came from, even if it wasn't perfect.

My original journey to retrace Steve Bloomer's footsteps had begun with his early years, growing up in Pear Tree. But as I made my way through Normanton I knew that I would eventually have to visit the place where he had died and also his final resting place at Nottingham Road Cemetery.

On Tuesday, October 16th by sheer coincidence I had an interview lined up to sign up as a supply teacher for Supply Desk at the Sun Inn Hotel on Nottingham Road. As this hotel was on the same road as Nottingham Road Cemetery I decided to pay it a visit after my interview concluded. I had no idea at all as to where I should start looking for Steve Bloomer's grave. Fortunately, I noticed an employee close by and asked him if he could help me find the grave. As soon as I had asked the question he stopped what he was doing and then kindly led me to the grave. Steve Bloomer's grave was a short walk from the entrance and not too far from a wooden bench inscribed in his memory. As soon as I laid eyes on it I noticed how new it looked compared to all the others around it, even though Bloomer had passed away nearly 70 years previously. I thanked the employee for assisting me. 'It's my pleasure, I do it quite regularly when visitors come to pay their respects to him', he replied.

I stood and looked down at the final resting place of the great Steve Bloomer, who was buried with his wife Sarah and two of his four daughters. An inscription on the headstone also remembered his two other daughters.

A Football Legend...   ...And His
Family
STEVE BLOOMER
England, Derby County & Middlesbrough
Who Died in 1938   Aged 64
His Wife
SARAH
And Their Daughters
Violet & Pat

And In Loving Memory Of
Their Other Children

HETTY & DORIS
Laid To Rest Elsewhere

The reason the headstone looked so new was because the current headstone was a replacement for the original. The new polished black marble was provided by his grandson Steve Richards in the 1990s, after the original stone grave and surround had fallen into a state of disrepair.

I stayed beside the grave for a while whilst also noticing a white marble grave close by that was dedicated to his parents, Caleb and Merab as well as his younger brother Phillip Bloomer. All three had died between 1887 and 1919.

As I looked into the distance I realised that Steve Bloomer's final resting place lay on a rise, watching over the whole of Derby. A point from where you could look out to Pride Park Stadium and the former Baseball Ground. Also close to Derby County F.C.'s original home, which was now the County Cricket Ground, where Bloomer had made both his home debut for the Rams and his England debut against Ireland.

I took some photos then made my way home. It was good to see his name again.

On Wednesday, October 17th I decided to pay a visit to the pub where Steve Bloomer had died on Saturday, April 16th 1938. I had found this information within Peter Seddon's book. As I didn't drink alcohol I took my friend Sib Hayer along with me for company.

Steve Bloomer: The Story of Football's First Superstar

'As he installed himself once more into the familiar surroundings of 19 Junction Street, Bloomer's family and the people of Derby had every reason to share that optimism but, as all football followers know, the closing stages of the game can deliver the cruellest of blows.'

As we entered the pub I made sure to have a good look around before we sat down. I quickly noticed a few Derby County F.C. jerseys and pictures on the walls, but nothing really indicated that Steve Bloomer had once lived here, although, I did spot a small picture of Steve Bloomer amongst one group of pictures. After we looked around for a bit we chatted to a regular who was sat alone. I'd brought

Peter Seddon's book with me and showed him the page where it said that Steve Bloomer had died in the pub. He was quite surprised at the revelation. We then ordered some drinks and I began to make conversation with a lady at the bar. I told her that we had come into have a word with the landlord to ask some questions about a famous footballer who had once lived in this building. She then told me that Sharon, the landlady, wasn't in today and then asked who the footballer was. On telling her about Steve Bloomer she was quite taken aback. She had no idea who Steve Bloomer was nor his connection to the old pub she now worked in. She did tell us that she would pass this information onto the landlady when she next saw her though. Sib and I then finished off our drinks and I told her that I might come back in again another time.

On the drive home, Sib asked me what I was going to do next. I wasn't sure but after three days of following the footsteps of Steve Bloomer all over Normanton and Derby I told Sib that I needed to show more for my efforts. I still wanted his name to be spoken and I didn't want to leave the trail cold at the pub. Steve Bloomer just would not leave my mind.

In 1988, around the time I first came across Steve Bloomer's name, The Pet Shop Boys released 'Always on my mind' a song that I absolutely loved and still do to this day in all its different versions. Elvis, Willie Nelson et al. This song always took me back home. At the time I remember my father had brought me a copy of the Derby Evening Telegraph, which included a large centre-page poster of the Pet Shop Boys.

Later that evening I uploaded all the photos I had taken to my recently created Facebook Group called 'Pear Tree - Derbyshire - England Residents Association'. I also added extra information to the Bloomer-related photos, which I had taken from Peter Seddon's book.

On Thursday, October 18th I woke up early once again and immediately jumped straight onto my PC to check my various notifications. I had by now added a few friends on Facebook and added new information to the various groups I had set up. It felt good to be reconnecting with the world again having spent the last year and a half in absolute isolation trying to avoid everyone and everything.

Over the next few hours I reflected on all that I had found out in the last few days. I had visited nearly every place on my list from Peter Seddon's book and thought about Steve Bloomer's life constantly. I decided I needed to share my enthusiasm and my stories. There was only one place in Derby to turn to do such a thing and connect to a bigger audience. My fellow Derby folk needed to know about the life of Steve Bloomer. It was not fair to forget any good person after their death.

In the afternoon I sat down at my PC and decided to write an email to the *Derby Evening Telegraph.*

Subject: Steve Bloomer's Watching Your Pint.

Hello, this is going to seem a bit random but I would just like to share something with you, I am a Pear Tree resident (Derby) and I have been living at 160 Portland Street for the last 28 years of my life. Recently, whilst reading the biography of the legendary Derby County footballer Steve Bloomer (Steve Bloomer: The Story of Football's First Superstar) I was amazed to find out that he actually used to live on my street at number 35 Portland Street.

I spent some time the other day going around the streets of Pear Tree taking photos of properties that were once lived in and/or rented/owned by Steve Bloomer and family. I have now uploaded all the photos on to my Facebook group: Pear Tree - Derbyshire - England Residents Association.

I also went to visit his grave at Nottingham Road Cemetery and talked to a member of staff there about him, as well as taking pictures of his grave and his parents, Caleb and Merab.

To finish off my day, yesterday, my friend and I went to visit the place where he supposedly died, 19 Junction Street, a.k.a The Great Northern Inn. In 1938 Steve Bloomer's daughter was a licensee of the pub, and he decided to move in with her after the death of his wife in 1936. The pub itself was quite a pleasant place with a few Derby County shirts on the wall and a few photos of past Derby Players including Steve Bloomer incidentally.

Anyway my point is this, I had a word with the lady behind the bar about whether she knew that Steve Bloomer had died there but she did not really know who he was. So I was told to ask a customer, he did not know either; I showed him my book to prove that this did seem to be the last place that Steve Bloomer resided. Upon leaving I asked the lady behind the bar and the other customer if they could pass on my little story to the landlady. Hopefully she might do something about it, but if she does not, do you think that somebody at the Derby Evening Telegraph could. To make sure that the whole of Derby recognises who Steve Bloomer was and what he did for our people. Surely there should be some kind of tribute to him there. A big picture on the wall or something. I know it was all a 100 years ago but he was a Pear Tree boy just like me and he deserves the recognition. So far in Derby, all we have is the memorial at the Lock-Up Yard that his own Grandson and family had to pay for.

Thank you
Kal.

I sent the email off not knowing if I would ever get a reply. But at least I had tried. What's the worst that could have happened? They could ignore it. It was better to try and fail than never try at all and then forever wonder what could have been.

After sending the email I began to get very anxious and disheartened at the possibility of never hearing anything back. I also began to become quite sad thinking about all the troubles and heartache Steve Bloomer had experienced in his life, especially his incarceration at Ruhleben and then his eventual death in 1938,

My greatest sadness about his life was not the FA Cups or the league titles that he so narrowly missed out on. My greatest sadness was for his family. The family he had left behind in Pear Tree. After retiring as a player Steve Bloomer went to Germany in July 1914 to coach Britannia Berlin 92. However within three weeks of arriving, World War I broke out. On Friday, 6th November 1914, he was arrested in the Spandau district of Berlin and then sent to the Ruhleben civilian detention camp where he was interned in Barrack 1.

This period of Steve Bloomer's life was tainted by death. A death of a loved one that nearly made him give up on life altogether.

After returning home to Pear Tree after more than three years of internment in Ruhleben he shared his experiences with the *The Post - Sunday Special* on Sunday, December 1st 1918.

'Only one fact mars the complete joy of my homecoming, and that is that since my departure from Derby for Berlin my second daughter, Violet, died during my term of internment in Ruhleben. She was a dear, lovable girl, of about eighteen years of age, and, although Mrs. Bloomer had several times written and said that she was ill, I was quite unprepared for the shock of the news of her death.

This occurred about April, 1917, and the fateful letter reached me at Ruhleben on May 5. At the time I was seated in a deck chair, enjoying a book and the spring sunshine, when Fred Pentland came up and tossed a letter into my lap. "From home, Steve," he remarked cheerfully.

I opened it, and the shock, as the import of the message dawned upon me, just about put me out.

After that I got rather low-spirited, and a sort of hopeless feeling that I should never survive the ordeal of captivity began to get a grip on me.

For a month I shunned everyone and everything, and was drifting to a fatal state of melancholy, when my football chums intervened.

"One thing is sure," said Percy Hartley, "and that is that you must start playing."

I protested, but it was of no avail. The whole bunch would hear of nothing else but that I must turn out again, and I was simply forced to do it.

Now I am glad that those real pals of mine were so insistent, because had I cut myself adrift from all interests I feel certain now that my reason would have gone.'

The death of his beloved daughter Violet Pretoria Bloomer had nearly destroyed him. But thankfully, it was his love of football that once again came to his rescue.

Steve Bloomer's lasting recollection of those lost years was poignantly lyrical:

'In Ruhleben we were all brothers. We made a life for ourselves out of nothing. We will always share a kinship and never forget. There were some terrible times. Make no mistake that boys became men in Ruhleben. But it is far more pleasant to recall the good times when we went out to play cricket and football. Those were the days when men became boys again.'

Another particular passage in Peter Seddon's biography really touched and tugged at my heart, as I remembered Steve Richards childhood account of the passing of his grandfather. It struck home so profoundly that Steve Richards words cut me like a knife and left a lasting mark.

Steve Bloomer: The Story of Football's First Superstar

'Final Whistle

Health is a fickle customer. The day after his return, while Derby County were winning 2-0 at Leeds United with goals from Ronnie Dix and Sammy Crooks, the newly rejuvenated Bloomer was taken ill at home. Whether it was a change in climate, or perhaps a delayed type of exhaustive reaction to what had been an incredible schedule, we will never know. What we do know is that Bloomer started to struggle more severely with bronchial trouble again, but there was every reason to believe that medication would turn the tide. Three weeks later, though, on the morning of 16 April, he had another more serious relapse and as his breathing became more laboured, his eight-year-old grandson Steve was hastily dispatched from his grandpop's room to fetch medical help. Now nearly 70, Steve Richards remembers that trauma still:

"The fastest I ever ran was to the doctor's house on the morning Steve Bloomer lay dying at my mother's home…but it was too late."

If it is true that our lives pass before us in the final moments, how much harder it must have been for Bloomer than the rest of us to edit the highlights; which of his special goals might he have recalled, which of the many countries he'd visited or the hundreds of fellow professionals he'd played against? Or perhaps he saw the broken bodies of Ibrox 1902, thought of England and recalled the stench of Ruhleben Camp on the day of his arrival. Or maybe his mind filled with the good times of games played and won, friends made, baseball, cricket, fishing, Spanish almond blossom … and young lads on the parks of Derby playing their hearts out to impress the old 'un just that once. Surely, too, he must have reflected on Sarah and the girls, his brothers and sisters, father and mother… and Derby County. We can only guess … perhaps he was just a small boy again shooting at sticks.

Steve Bloomer was a tough man who had overcome many obstacles but the opponents ranged against him that morning, later written into their allotted spaces by Eric Johnson MRCS, were the hardest of them all. Stephen

Bloomer, male, 64 years, retired professional footballer, finally met his match in the face of myocardial failure, asthma, bronchitis and myocardial degeneration. He never did get to see Derby County again, or the Cup Final ... how strange that having seen or played in a game every week in season for 50 years, he should not see a single match in his final six months.

It was a Saturday, the day when he had always been so much more alive than any other; but on this Saturday there was no chaff and banter, no cartwheels and lusty cheers, no triumphal band playing in his honour and no way out of the dark tunnel that faced him. Instead, an elderly gent with a life full of memories closed his eyes on the world for the final time ... the 'Incomparable Steve' was dead.

The death of Steve Bloomer saddened me, all over again. Just as it had done the very first time I had come across his name some 20 years previously. But this time I knew exactly how his passing would have felt to his immediate family having lost my own father too. I felt their pain for real. I didn't want my father forgotten and I was quite certain now that the same applied to Bloomer and his legacy too.

Steve Richards was, by now, coming towards the last years of his life; maybe he still could pay the ultimate mark of gratitude to his beloved grandfather. He had worked tirelessly all his life to keep the memory of Steve Bloomer alive and kicking, but maybe now it was time for someone else to join him and continue to carry the legacy on. Peter Seddon had already done a great job with his biography. But what if I could also somehow contribute?

'Et lux tenebris lucet'
'And the light shineth in the darkness'

The next afternoon I was sitting down at my PC in the front room thinking about how I could try to share Steve Bloomer's story with an even wider audience. But at the same time I was also juggling with the idea that I wanted to do something for my father too.

At the time, I definitely had an urge to write, but there was no point writing about Steve Bloomer again. Peter Seddon, had already done a great job with his own written biography. And there was no point in me writing about my father alone, as surely nobody would ever want to read a book about his suicide. I began to feel quite miserable at the predicament I now found myself in. On the one hand I wanted to write about a Pear Tree legend and then on the other hand I wanted to write about my father. Yet, I couldn't do either of them separately, because I felt that it just wouldn't work. Nothing was going my way. As I sat at my desk my head sunk low as I brought my hands down over my knees and then clasped them together. I was then strangely drawn to the bookcase that was built into my wall. As I looked up I caught a glimpse of a wonderful book I'd purchased and read a year previously called *My Father And Other Working Class Football Heroes* by Gary Imlach.

As soon as the title of that book came into my mind I felt within me an intense reaction I had never experienced before. One moment I was sat cold and glum and then in the next moment I felt a warm fuzzy sensation within me that spread quickly throughout my body as if a light had been switched on for the very first time. I was now standing, almost floating, and this feeling remained for a good few seconds as I tried to come to terms with what had just happened to me. It felt like a regeneration surge. That is the only way I could describe it. There was my sign. There was my answer. To what? I didn't quite know, but I knew it felt right. I had identified with something and I knew I had to pursue it no matter what. I had to persevere because there was definitely something good that was waiting for me on the other side. I now had a purpose. And it was obvious that Steve Bloomer would no doubt play a significant part in that journey. But still, I wasn't quite sure exactly how.

On Friday, October 19th I'd made plans with Rav to make an early morning visit to Waterstones in the town centre. A couple of days previously Marcus Shukla, an old Mackworth college friend had informed me that a group of Derby County legends would be appearing at the bookstore for a book signing. The book was called *Right Place Right Time; The Inside Story of Clough's Derby Days* by George Edwards.

By the time Rav and I got there they were still setting up the tables and chairs, and we were the first ones in the queue. As we waited in line I saw the author of the book, George Edwards take his seat followed by Willie Carlin, John O'Hare, Alan Durban and finally Roy McFarland. As I watched on I couldn't believe what I was seeing. On the Sunday before, I had managed to collect the autographs of the legendary Kevin Hector and Roger Davies and now here I was amongst even more legends of Derby County F.C.

When my chance to meet them all finally arrived, I made sure to greet them all with a smile and a handshake. George Edwards signed his book and then I once again pulled out my copy of *The Who's Who of Derby County* by Gerald Mortimer. I began with Willie Carlin and asked if he could sign it first. He gratefully did so then shook my hand with one of the strongest handshakes I had ever experienced in my life. I then asked the same of Alan Durban, then John O'Hare. I finally passed my book over to Roy McFarland. He leafed through it as I told him about meeting Kevin Hector and Roger Davies in the previous week. I also told him about the time I once saw him outside Derby Train Station, but I was unable to get his autograph. He smiled then happily signed his autograph next to his profile and picture in the book. I was over the moon. As all this was happening Rav was taking pictures in the background. It had been an unbelievable week. In the first 29 years of my life I hadn't met any of these heroes of mine and then in the space of a week I had met nearly half of Clough and Taylor's original Derby County F.C. old boys.

After I managed to gain all their autographs I stepped back and stood next to Rav smiling, as I showed her all the autographs I had collected in the last few days. I was so pleased with myself. As soon as I found out about all these players showing up at their various events I made the effort to go out and see them, to make sure I met them and to also ask for their autographs. A couple of years previously I would never had had the courage to do so, but all that changed with the death of my father. I was never again going to miss out on these opportunities to add happiness into my life. No matter how small it may have seemed to others. I would never let the fear of failure or nerves get the better of me again. Life was too short and I knew I had to make the best of what I had. I had met some of my greatest heroes in life and I was happy.

When Rav and I got back home to Pear Tree, I placed the book on my desk next to my PC. Still smiling I switched on the PC and then logged into my Hotmail account. I immediately noticed an email from the *Derby Evening Telegraph* waiting for me in my inbox. It could only be about one thing and one person only.

The next day I would be on my way back to the Great Northern Inn.

Steve Bloomer was calling.

Chapter 18: The Great Northern

Shaun Jepson, a reporter at the *Derby Evening Telegraph* had replied to the email I'd sent to the newspaper a couple of days previously.

Hi there,
With regards to the email you sent to us, can you call me or email your details so I can speak to you?
Best wishes,
Shaun Jepson
Abbey, Arboretum and Normanton Reporter

I immediately felt a feeling of great excitement, which quickly transformed into anxiety when I then realised that I would have to make a phone call and talk to Shaun in person. As apprehensive as I was I knew I had to do it as quickly as possible to alleviate my worries. So, I picked up my mobile and carefully dialled the number Shaun had supplied so that I could get back in touch with him.

On getting through to Shaun, I excitedly explained to him reason I wanted to share the Steve Bloomer story; how after reading Peter Seddon's biography I had been so completely captivated by the life of a local legend. A life story I believed needed to be reclaimed and shared with the people of Derby.

At no point during this call did I mention my father, his death or how he had died. I guess I was just too worried that my father's suicide might also be added into an article should one be ever written up. I was obviously still fearful of what people might think or say about me or my father. I couldn't risk it. It was still too early for me to completely open up even though my engagement on Facebook had unlocked many more doors in my life. I wanted this story to be entirely about Steve Bloomer.

Having taken some more notes whilst chatting to me on the phone, Shaun then asked me if I could meet the *Derby Evening Telegraph* photographer, Ian Hodgkinson at the Great Northern Inn on the following day. Shaun also mentioned that the landlady Sharon would also be there to greet me.

On Saturday, October 20th I made a return visit to the Great Northern Inn Pub. Once again I asked my friend Sib to come along with me and we arrived at the pub about half an hour before I was supposed to. As we waited in the car I kept looking back over my shoulder at the entrance to see if I could spot anyone coming in or out. As I did so I held tight onto the books I had brought along with me. The last time I was at the pub I saw very little Steve Bloomer related memorabilia on the walls. So on this occasion I made sure to bring some books along with me that contained pictures of Steve Bloomer within them. The two books were Peter Seddon's biography and *The Who's Who of Derby County* by Gerald Mortimer. I also decided to wear my new DCFC Polo training shirt that I had bought the day before.

After a few more minutes waiting around in the car we decided to enter the pub. As we walked in we noticed Sharon the landlady standing behind the bar. She immediately approached Sib and I after realising who we were. She then asked us to take a seat at one of the tables and then ordered us all a drink. She had by now already been informed about Steve Bloomer, but had no idea he had once lived in the pub, nor that it was also the place where he had died. I filled her in on some more information I had found out from Peter Seddon's biography. After a few minutes, Ian, the photographer, entered the pub and as he was setting his equipment up for the photo shoot he continued to engage in conversation with us all.

When he was ready for us, he asked Sharon and I to lean over the bar from opposite sides and then look straight into the camera. As I did so I held down one book open and flat against the surface of the bar. With my other hand I held up Peter Seddon's book, so that Steve Bloomer's picture on the front cover was facing towards the camera. Sharon And I were then asked to go outside and have some more photos taken with the pub sign in view. Once again Peter Seddon's book was used as a prop as well as a picture frame that had been taken off a wall, which had pictures of some ex Derby County F.C. footballers on it.

It had been the first time in my life that I had ever experienced anything like this. But I was happy to have my photos taken even though the main reason for being there that day was really to show off my pictures of Steve Bloomer and Peter Seddon's biography.

When all the photography was complete Ian asked me for my full name and asked that I spell it out for him. He then left us all to travel onto his next job. As all this was happening, Sib had been playing pool with one of the regulars. Sib had also been filling him in on what I was up to. As I went over to pool table the man Sib was playing against seemed very pleased with what I was doing. He then also mentioned to us that he was a distant relation of Bert Mozley, another ex England international who also played for Derby County F.C. As Sib and I were about to leave, the man shook my hand and then said to me, 'Don't take offence but why are you … why are you even doing this?' I didn't take offence. It was obvious why he was asking; 'Why did it matter to people like me? Why did I care?' He was obviously not being malicious or anything. It was a legitimate question. I thought about it for a short moment then replied, 'I'm doing this for Steve Bloomer. He was a Pear Tree boy just like me and I will not let him be forgotten. He deserves to be remembered'. Sib and I then said our farewells to everybody in the pub. I couldn't stop smiling to myself all the way home.

Later in the afternoon I sat down at my PC to send Shaun another email.

Had a great day today, luckily I brought all my books, so we got some good pictures. Had a long chat with the landlady too and she is very pleased. Trying to get hold of a bloke at DCFC media now, amazingly, he is the father of another guy I met on Facebook, who joined my 'Brian Clough and Peter Taylor Appreciation Society' Group. Hoping to get him on board to maybe provide the pub with stuff? I think the

landlady might have Steve Richards contact details too.......Bloomer's Grandson.
Kal.

P.S
Created another group too........
Steve Bloomer's Watching your Pint at the Great Northern Inn

The next day on Sunday, October 21st Rav and I decided to visit her brother in Wigston, Leicester. As I was driving, I just could not stop thinking about all the things that I had experienced in the last few days. My life had literally turned upside down, but in a good way. From a point where I was not engaging with anyone to a point where I was now having my photo taken for an article that might be written up about my great hero Steve Bloomer in the local newspaper. It was all quite surreal.

So many things were now turning over in my mind that I was becoming lost in my own little world trying to process them all. My mind was working on overdrive. Suddenly my thoughts quickly turned to the fact that in the next couple of days there would be a high possibility that an article about me would be appearing in my local newspaper. Now a week, a month or even a year before, this would have filled me with enormous dread. But not now, this was different as I would be appearing alongside my great hero and it would be a positive story that would hopefully make people happy and fill them with a sense of pride. It was definitely making me happy, knowing that I may make others happy too. I had turned a corner in my life. Steve Bloomer would be spoken about again by Derby folk and I was happy to know that I had played a small part in that.

As I continued to think about all this another thought came into my mind that shook everything up entirely. I thought back to the day I felt that intense 'regeneration' surge. I thought back to how it made me feel. I thought back to what made me feel that way. The book, *My Father And Other Working Class Heroes* and then the answer hit me. The revelation had come to me the other day, but I just couldn't work out what it meant at the time other than knowing that Steve Bloomer had a part to play in it. The moment of realisation made me whisper the words 'The Lost Legend of Pear Tree' and I smiled. 'You what?' asked Rav. 'My Father & The Lost Legend of Pear Tree', I replied. 'What does that mean?', asked Rav. 'It means that I'm going to write a story. I'm going to write a book about my dad and Steve Bloomer'.

In that moment I had realised what my life now held for me after the passing of my father. Completing my story, finishing my book and then publishing it would be the ultimate act of pure satisfaction and achievement. It would keep me busy, it would keep me distracted. It would give me a purpose. To kick on. To keep busy living. To keep the memories alive.

Most of all though, I knew that I would be doing it for my father. I would write a book, not just about my father but the link to Steve Bloomer and my old neighbourhood of Pear Tree in Derby. In the process I would make something positive come out of his death. Suicide would not stop me or the world from sharing my father's story and talking about him.

As we continued to drive towards Wigston, in my mind I had already begun putting the story together. As we arrived at Rav's brother's house, I was in my own little world; excited, nervous, and overflowing with energy.

A few minutes after entering the house my mobile phone began to ring. I would have normally ignored it, but something inside me made me answer it. It was Shaun, I answered it immediately and he then asked me how I was. I told him I was fine and that I was currently in Leicester. He then told me that the Steve Bloomer story would be published in the *Derby Evening Telegraph* over the next day or so. My heartbeat quickened. It was so great to hear and I felt justified. I had what I thought was a good story and I just went with it. And it had paid off. Steve Bloomer was going to be in the local paper again. Possibly for the first time in a very long time.

My heart was now racing; I was already very excited before the phone call, so I decided to tell Shaun that there was more to the story than I had initially let on. There was another important reason why I originally went searching for Steve Bloomer. It had a significant link to my late father and I would explain it all to him via an email when I got back home from Leicester.

Later in the evening I sat down at my PC and began to write a very long email to Shaun.

I began the email by informing Shaun that my Steve Bloomer story was now developing and that there was a greater backstory to it all that included my father. I then revealed to Shaun that my father had tragically passed away a year and a half previously after having experienced depression on and off for many years.

At this point I had still not used the word suicide. Maybe I just didn't know how to put it across and bring it up in conversation. I had already realised from experience how the word could be such a cruel conversation killer when you were talking about the loss of life due to suicide.

I then began telling Shaun about what I was up to in my life at the time that my father had passed away and how my father's death had continued to affect my own life. I explained my time at John Port School after the death of my father and how his death had impacted on every part of my life ever since. I also mentioned the obituary that the *Derby Evening Telegraph* published after his death too. As well as the significance of the quote I had put in it.

My journey to find Steve Bloomer was in essence my journey to find my father as well as myself. And in the process make sure that neither of them was forgotten. No good father should ever be forgotten I told him.

I also explained my current position in terms of my life and work. I had recently signed up with a teaching supply agency and was hoping to start work in December whilst also continuing to train to become a driving instructor. I was also now assisting with coaching the GAD Khalsa Sports Under 12s Boys Football Team who were based at the Guru Arjan Dev Gurdwara, Derby.

At the end of my long rambling, spelling mistake littered email I effectively told Shaun, in my excited state, that I would be writing my whole story up and begin it straightaway. I ended the email by thanking Shaun for following up my original Steve Bloomer story, which then inevitably led me to the decision to become a writer. I was going to bring the legend of Pear Tree back home and all I had to do now, was write it.

Much later in the evening Shaun replied.

That's quite a story mate. Well done for coming through everything, I'm sure your father would be very proud. Keep in touch and let me know how things go.

By the time Shaun had replied back to me I was already in the process of completing the first chapter. The real story of the search for Steve Bloomer had begun. My father's suicide had become a cathartic catalyst to write and share his story.

That evening I had opened up my laptop and sat down alone in the living room. I then began to write down the title of my story.

My Father & The Lost Legend of Pear Tree

Chapter 1: D Day

It was Wednesday, March 1st 2006 and life was great.

From the moment I began typing I could not stop writing for about five hours solid. The first chapter was now almost complete and I just kept going. In the process of writing my story I had gone through nearly every emotion; sadness, laughter, anguish and much more as the tears freely flowed over my cheeks. I had not cried like this for a long while, nor had I laughed in equal measure. As I remembered all the things my father and I had shared between us, over the years and the smiles that came with it. Writing had allowed the memories of my father to be reclaimed from the furthest reaches of my mind where they had become almost impenetrable for so long.

My father was a decent gentle man yet people had stopped talking about him. In my opinion this was entirely because of the way he had tragically died. It was obvious to me now that people didn't mention him in fear of upsetting me, or possibly upsetting themselves too. Writing my story about my father would allow people to talk about him again and therefore also allow him to be remembered again. Appearing in the *Derby Evening Telegraph* would be the first step on my journey. People knowing my name and knowing that I lived in Pear Tree would open the door for me. Steve Bloomer would be the man who kicked it all off in my quest to reclaim my father. However, this all depended on the outcome of the *Derby Evening Telegraph* article.

That night I typed like my life depended on it, as the memories continued to pour out of me and onto my laptop screen. Sometimes I would lose them as quickly as I had remembered them. At this stage I was now becoming very tired and I knew that the sun would be rising soon. It was time to get some sleep as in a few hours it could be the big day, or it could be nothing at all. I then saved all that I had typed up and then crashed into bed absolutely exhausted.

Chapter 19: Steve Bloomer's Watching

It was Monday, October 22nd 2007 and I had just awoken from my sleep. I looked at the time on my watch and realised that I'd only been asleep for about four hours. I'd spent the majority of last night writing. I was drained, feeling really low and still absolutely exhausted. I hadn't felt like this since the very dark days after the passing of my father. 'Was my body trying to tell me something again? Was it preparing me for another life changing event?', I thought to myself. Writing was now the last thing on my mind. And then I remembered. The *Derby Evening Telegraph*. Today could be the day. The day that Steve Bloomer is in the paper. The day I'm in the paper. I leapt out of my bed and quickly boot up my PC to check to see if I could find the story on the *This Is Derbyshire* website. Unfortunately there was nothing there. I got dressed and carried out my daily morning grooming routines. Afterwards, I then decided to go out for a little walk. I needed to clear my mind and stretch my legs. There was no time to eat as usual, but that was the norm in the mornings for me. On top of that, nervous energy began coursing through my body and my stomach began to flutter. The story might not have appeared online yet, but it could be in the print edition of the newspaper. There was only one way to find out.

Within minutes I was walking out of my house on Portland Street and heading towards my mamma's old shop on Balfour Road. I had also decided to bring my camera along with me just incase.

I really didn't know what to expect, but I thought I'd better buy the paper anyway. 'You never know, there might be a tiny piece about Steve Bloomer within it'. On walking into the shop I looked around for the *Derby Evening Telegraph* but I couldn't see any. So I made my way to the counter to ask the lady serving where I could buy a copy. But just as I was about to ask the question, I noticed a few of them piled up neatly on top of the counter. I looked up at the lady but then immediately looked back down at one of the newspapers. In the corner of the newspaper I had recognised a familiar face staring right back at me. 'Oh my goodness', I thought to myself. The incomparable Steve Bloomer was watching me.

'I've done it', I whispered to myself. I moved closer toward the counter and began reading the headline; 'The pub that was home to a Rams legend'. To the left of the headline was a picture of myself and Sharon, outside the Great Northern Inn and just to the right of it under the headline; 'Landlady's Bloomer surprise: Page 5'.

'I'll take two of these please. I'm on page 5 you know', I said to the lady. 'Really, what have you been up to then?', she asked. 'Oh, nothing bad, I found Steve Bloomer', I replied. We then both picked up a newspaper and flicked to page 5. Nearly the whole page was dedicated to the story. 'Well done' said the lady having recognised that it was me in the picture. I hurriedly paid for the newspapers as another customer had come in and began talking to the lady. Smiling from ear to ear, I bid her goodbye and shot straight out of the door, filled with happiness.

On leaving the shop I began walking towards Sainsbury's in the hope of buying more copies of the newspaper, but then realised that I already had two on me. I couldn't walk in there with two in my hand and then try to buy another two or three more. It would all get quite confusing trying to explain why I wanted to buy so many. So I decided to go home. As I walked back down Portland Street I flicked to page 5 again and then began reading the article in its entirety.

Landlady to pump up the tributes to legend at her pub

Licensee seeking memorabilia of Rams goal scorer Steve Bloomer.

Monday, October 22nd, 2007 – *The Derby Telegraph*

By Shaun Jepson.

A Derby landlady has vowed to fill her pub with Steve Bloomer memorabilia after she discovered that the Derby County legend had once lived there.

Sharon Morgan said that she was astounded to discover that Bloomer – who scored 332 goals in 525 appearances for the Rams – used to live in the Great Northern Inn, in Junction Street.

Bloomer lived there in 1936 while his daughter was the pub licensee.

Lifelong Rams fan Kalwinder Singh Dhindsa told Mrs Morgan about her pub's famous association during a visit.

He made the discovery while reading Bloomer's biography, Steve Bloomer: The story of Football's First Superstar.

An entry in the book by Steve Richards, Bloomer's grandson, recorded that Derby's greatest-ever goal scorer died in the pub in 1938.

Mrs Morgan, 50 has held the license at the pub for two years. She said "I was a bit surprised at first because it wasn't something I'd heard before.

I was asking the locals about it because they're all big Derby fans and they didn't seem to know either.

I've got a few Derby pieces on the walls and a couple of pictures of Steve Bloomer because I'm trying to build up the Derby theme for my regulars.

I'd like to get some really nice pieces of memorabilia now I know this because it's really exciting."

Mr Dhindsa of Portland Street, said that he was amazed to learn from the book that Bloomer also lived in the street where he now lives.

"I'm a big Derby County fan and when I read that he lived on my street, I couldn't believe it," said Mr Dhindsa, 28.

"After reading that in the book I spent some time going around the streets of Pear Tree taking photos of properties that were once lived in, rented or owned by Steve Bloomer and his family.

I also went to visit his grave at Nottingham Road cemetery and talked to a member of staff there about him, as well as taking pictures of his grave and of his parents, Caleb and Merab.

I think it is important to make sure that the whole of Derby recognizes who Steve Bloomer was and what he did for our people."

Steve Bloomer is regarded as Derby County's number one all-time legend.

Fans dedicated a song to him and players emerge from the Pride Park tunnel on to the pitch at every home game to the tune of Steve Bloomer's Watching – ringing out from 30,000 fans.

The £525,000 Astro-Turf football pitches on the Racecourse, off St Mark's Road were named after Bloomer last year.

And the plans for a £20M plaza development at Pride Park include monuments of the Rams striker.

Mr Dhindsa said that more needed to be done to recognize Bloomer's achievements.

"I know it was all of 100 years ago, but he was a Pear Tree boy just like me and he deserves the recognition', he said.

So far in Derby, all we have is the memorial at the Lock-Up Yard, in Corn Market, and his own family had to pay for that."

By the time I had reached Pear Tree Crescent I had read the whole page. I then looked up at the photos again at the top of the article with myself and Sharon. Underneath it was written: Our Hero: Kal Dhindsa and Sharon Morgan.

Amazing! Shaun had done a wonderful job. I felt so proud. So proud that Steve Bloomer had been remembered and that people would now know that he was also a local lad from Pear Tree too. A local lad like myself; a local lad just like my father. What a magnificent feeling to have experienced just as I passed Pear Tree Crescent in the heart of Pear Tree.

As soon as I got home I logged back onto my PC and searched for the story on the *This Is Derbyshire* website. Once again, I caught sight of Steve Bloomer staring right back at me. It was done. I had done it. Steve Bloomer was back in the Derby news.

Having found the link to the story on the website I decided to share it on Facebook with a status update: 'Kalwinder is Amazed. He is on page 1 and 5 of the *Derby Evening Telegraph*. I did it LOL'.

I also decided to email Shaun and thank him for producing such a great piece and how my father would have been very proud. I then decided to text a few people including Sharon, Rav and my friend Tim Fearn about the story in the paper.

When texting Tim all I said was that he should have a look at today's paper as I was in it in relation to Derby County F.C. 'You are famous! Are you with some legends?' he replied. 'Yes, Steve Bloomer you could say. Tell the students at school', I replied.

After I sent off a flurry of emails and texts my hunger finally caught up with me. So, I decided to once again leave the house and this time head down towards Sainsbury's to buy some more papers and maybe something to eat.

As I entered Sainsbury's I headed towards the alcohol and tobacco section where the *Derby Evening Telegraph* was sold. As I approached the stand I could see the day's edition on every shelf with Steve Bloomer's face on every copy.

It was a great thing to see so I decided to take a couple of photos of the stand. I then went off to buy some food, but ended up picking up a drink instead. As I made my way back to the news stand I decided to take some more pictures but this time with me in them standing next to the newspapers or even reading one, but to do this I required someone to do me a favour. As I stood there for a few seconds trying to find someone a member of staff walked past me. 'Excuse me, but this is going to sound a bit weird but I'm on page 1 and 5 of the *Derby Evening Telegraph*. Could you please take some pictures of me posing with it?', I asked. The lady laughed, 'Of course I will'. So, I placed the drink back on a shelf, then stood next to the news stand as I smiled back at the camera. I then thanked the lady for taking the pictures and joined the queue to pay for the items.

'Is that four newspapers?', the cashier asked. 'Yes. I'm in the paper you see', I replied. 'What for?', she asked. So once again I explained my search for Steve Bloomer.

The cashier then informed me that her daughter worked at Pride Park, as she then began to glance over the article. 'I'll have a read of this properly when I get home. I'll also make sure my husband reads it too', she then told me. 'Do you live near Junction Street?', she asked. 'No, I live down the road on Portland Street. Steve Bloomer used to live on that same street too', I replied.

After I paid for my newspapers and drink I made my way back down towards Portland Street. However, this time I was going to go down a bit further past my home. As I walked down the road, I began sipping at my drink in between smiles. My intention was to go all the way down to 35 Portland Street. But before that I would pass Steve Bloomer's old school building, which was now the Wallis clothing factory. I walked over to Stevenson Butchers and then noticed the owner John Culling through the window. 'Hello again, remember me? I was in the other day, asking questions about your family and Steve Bloomer', I said. Mr Culling did remember so I showed him one of my four copies of the *Derby Evening Telegraph*. 'I'm in the paper today. A story about Steve Bloomer. They've even mentioned that he was from Pear Tree just like us', I told him. Mr Culling then began looking over the article. 'You can keep that paper. Thank you for sharing your memories of your family and Steve Bloomer with me. I'm very grateful', I told him as I bid him goodbye.

As I walked out of the shop I looked back at the old façade. ESTD. 1885. F.T.Stevenson.73. John Culling was now the owner, his mother was a Stevenson before she got married. On the last occasion I had popped in Mr Culling had shown me a picture that was taken in the late nineteenth century of the front of the shop. He pointed out his mother's father and uncle. It really was a family butcher. There is no doubt that

Steve Bloomer and his family would have used it themselves many years previously.

35 Portland Street was just behind the old chemist and opposite The Jolly Fagman newsagent. As I stood outside Steve Bloomer's old family home on Portland Street, I raised a smile in acknowledgement for the Pear Tree old boy. I then walked back up St Thomas Road past the Pear Tree Inn Pub, past Terrys Butchers and then back down Pear Tree Crescent and home again.

Later on in the day I went to visit Sharon at the Great Northern Inn. She had also bought a copy of the newspaper and was just as happy as me with the article. As we sat and talked Sharon began telling me of her future plans for the pub and how she hoped to display more pictures of Steve Bloomer. I also let it be known to her that a couple of hours earlier I had emailed Derby County F.C. and asked if they could put me in touch with Jim Fearn who was Head of Media at the Club. The reason I contacted him was to find out what had happened to the original Steve Bloomer tablet from the old Baseball Ground and whether it was still in the Club's possession. Jim Fearn replied to my original request very promptly having read the link to the day's story in the newspaper as well as reading the original email I had sent to Shaun in relation to finding where Steve Bloomer had died. I was told that the tablet was in safe hands and still in the Club's possession and that it was hoped that in the future it would be displayed in a permanent museum within Pride Park. It was a great relief to me when I was told that the tablet was in safe hands and had not been lost or even stolen.

Jim Fearn had also been in touch with Sharon earlier in the day too. Sharon was very pleased with all the publicity generated for the pub as she really wanted business to pick up. I reassured her that the article could prompt fans to donate memorabilia to the pub too. But if she really wanted to make something great to come out of this story, then she must try and get hold of Steve Richards, Steve Bloomer's grandson. I told her that he must be in his late 70s now. Sharon then interrupted and told me that Jim Fearn had passed Steve Richards' phone number on to her earlier in the day. 'You must get him down', I excitedly told her.

I also needed to meet Steve Richards, his words of his grandfather's passing in Peter Seddon's Biography had touched me so much. I felt his sadness for the loss of his grandfather, just as I felt the sadness of my own father's passing. I wanted Steve Richards to return to the Great Northern Inn one final time. Steve Richards had worked tirelessly all his life to keep the memory of his grandfather alive. Maybe all these years later he could make one final ultimate mark of respect to his beloved grandfather. Maybe now it was time for someone else to carry that legacy on and for him to know that it would remain in safe hands. I needed to meet him.

On the way home from the pub I decided to pop into my big mamma's new shop on Boyer Street. Although his shop was selling the paper on the day he hadn't spotted me inside, as he hadn't yet read it. So, I showed him the front cover then directed him to page 5. He smiled as he saw a picture of me smiling back at him. 'That's my nephew you know?', he proudly told a customer waiting to be served.

The next day on Tuesday, October 23rd I once again went to the shop to buy the newspaper, on the chance that I might be in it again. I flicked through it all until I made my way to about 3 pages from the end, at which point I was once again stopped dead in my tracks. There staring straight back at me were my GAD Khalsa Under 12s; a team photo with all the coaching staff including myself. I had made the paper twice in two days. I could not help but laugh. I had well and truly shattered all my anxieties about appearing in the limelight of media.

Shaun Jepson and the *Derby Evening Telegraph* had cracked me open. Steve Bloomer had set me free. My goal to remember Steve Bloomer had well and truly been kicked off and the journey to reclaim my father had only just begun. My father would get his story and I would succeed. In the words of Sir Ernest Shackleton: 'Fortitudine Vincimus - By Endurance We Conquer'.

Personally, one story in the *Derby Evening Telegraph* about Steve Bloomer was great, but I knew deep down that something more significant had to be accomplished for his legacy to live on forever. A tribute was most definitely required and Derby County F.C. alluded to that in the article when they said that the club had a plan for a £20M plaza development at Pride Park that would include a monument of the Rams striker. My dream was still alive. Maybe I could still contribute to building something too.

*

When Brian Howard Clough passed away on Monday, September 20th 2004, a couple of days later I walked to Pride Park to leave a message in his book of condolence.

Never in the fields of the East Midlands will so much be owed by so many to such a man ever again. You did more than contribute, you brought hope and joy to us all.
RIP.
K S Dhindsa.

I wrote this little farewell message as a nod to the RAF and Churchill's 'The Few' speech, as Brian Clough also had a link to the RAF having carried out his national service with them. I also added the 'contribute' bit because Brian Clough once said the following about how he would like to be remembered.

'I want no epitaphs of profound history and all that type of thing. I contributed. I would hope they would say that, and I would hope somebody liked me.'

On Brian Clough's passing that quote really tugged at my heartstrings. He had done so much for my people in Derby and all I could do for him at the time was to write this little message expressing my deepest thanks. In my mind I continued to always hope that one day I could show him and his family what he really meant to all us Derby folk. I had plenty of ideas. I just didn't know how to accomplish them though.

I wrote the following on a forum message board a few weeks after his passing.

Written on the brianclough.com message board.
Quote (Khalis @ Oct. 30 2004,12:58)

You see things; and you say, 'Why?' But I dream things that never were; and I say, 'Why not?'
Shoeless Joe – W.P. Kinsella – Field of Dreams (Film).
George Bernard Shaw

I think a statue, as a memorial would be a great idea. There could be a statue of Mr Clough in each of the 3 main cities that he either played at or managed. For example, in Middlesbrough there could be a statue of him as a young man, a footballing legend in his playing days, then in Derby a statue, as he looked in his period at the Rams and then lastly a statue of Mr Clough when he managed Forest in his later years. A different statue for each period of his life.

I think the naming of the A52 is a good idea, but a fitting memorial should be one, where people can actively be involved in something worthwhile. The naming of the road is just a symbolic gesture. Maybe someone could organise charity events i.e. bike rides or distance runs to celebrate his life and his career and also raise money for charities in the process. This would involve the public and raise awareness for the charities.

Chapter 20: Pear Tree Ram

Later in the morning I met up with an old friend in town. As Tom Martin and I walked around the city centre I began to tell him about everything that I had been up to since we last met. I also revealed to him what I was hoping to achieve off the back of the Steve Bloomer article in terms of my own writing. At one point we even popped into the Derby fish market to see the memorial to Steve Bloomer.

Steve Richards had fought long and hard to have this memorial erected to his grandfather in the Lock-Up Yard. On the day of its unveiling former England forwards Tom Finney, Wilf Mannion and Nat Lofthouse were also present for the occasion of the unveiling.

Steve Bloomer, the first king of English football goal scorers, entered the 20th century with his fame as Derby County's outstanding marksman already established.
As the next century beckoned – when this monument was erected in 1996 – his Rams' all-games record of 332 goals was still unsurpassed.

His 353 Football League goals for Derby County and Middlesbrough was a record until near his death in 1938 at 64.

Bloomer's 28 goals in 23 games gave him a then unique average of 1.21 per cap.

The son of a Midlands' blacksmith, Bloomer was a pupil at St James' School in Derby.

He was described as a 'Working Class Hero' by Nottingham Trent University student Jonathan Belshaw in his 1990's study of Victorian social changes.

The monument erected through the auction of Bloomer's England caps, plus family contributions, has been presented to Derby City Council by his descendants.

As I read the inscription a few phrases stuck in my thoughts. '28 goals in 23 games', 'Working Class Hero' and then ultimately the last line about his family's contribution to the monument. I felt the lump of emotion in my throat grow bigger, 'That's not right Tom, that must be rectified. This city owes him much more'.

After visiting the memorial Tom and I decided to head towards the Assembly Rooms for something to eat and drink.

It was still early morning so as per usual I decided not to eat but opted instead for a hot chocolate. We had plenty of catching up to do, as we had not seen each other for a long while. It was good to have a laugh and smile again talking about our time together in Ashby-de-la-Zouch and Shepshed during our teaching placements. After we finished our drinks we decided to take a trip down to the Derby Heritage Centre.

As we were walking towards the Heritage Centre my mobile began to ring and I noticed that it was Sharon calling. I had texted her earlier in the day to ask if there had been any more developments regarding the Steve Bloomer story. On answering the call I was informed by Sharon that she had been in touch with Steve Richards and that he was very keen to help us gain more publicity for his late grandfather. However, it would be a bit difficult for him to get too involved at the moment because later in the week he would need to go into hospital for an operation.

Steve Richards was now in the later stages of his life and not in the best of health, having recently celebrated his 78th birthday.

I was so pleased that Steve Richards had read the story about my search for Steve Bloomer in the *Derby Evening Telegraph*. He also told Sharon that members of his extended family overseas had also read the article and were also very pleased that Steve Bloomer's legacy still lived on and was not forgotten, especially in Derby.

'We must get him down. He must come home to Derby'. I said to Sharon in great excitement.

After visiting the Derby Heritage Centre with Tom we then went our separate ways. As we said goodbye he told me how pleased he was to see me in such good spirits. He then also joked that I had chosen the wrong profession and should have followed him down his path and become a history teacher instead.

As I walked back towards my car I decided to quickly pop into Waterstones. After a few minutes hovering around the Derby section I left the store with a copy of Anton Rippon's *A Derby Boy*.

As I sat in my car I began to wonder, 'What if people now begin to recognise me in Derby? Recognised me for what though?'. Surely, if it was to make a connection to my father, Mohinder Singh Dhindsa. Then that is all that mattered. He would not be forgotten. That's all that mattered to me. To remember him was to also spread awareness of how he died. Maybe I could also try and help others bereaved by suicide. I still had a lot to understand and I knew it would take time. But time is something I had a lot of. Time was also now something that I would cherish, to live as long as possible to make up for all the years my father had missed out on.

As I was driving out of town I decided to pop in to The Great Northern Inn again to meet Sharon. She was now really excited about everything that had been going on in relation to the Steve Bloomer story. Earlier in the day a member of the public had brought her in a scanned postcard of Steve Bloomer and his England caps. The postcard had been given to the man by his godfather; the godfather himself, being Steve Bloomer. It was now clear to me that people still remembered and that people still cared as they offered up their stories and mementoes.

On the day of Steve Bloomer's death on Saturday, April 16th 1938, an eight-year-old Steve Richards watched on as his beloved grandfather took his final breath. Could it now be that 70 years later Steve Richards would return to The Great Northern Inn to celebrate the life of his legendary grandfather? 'What a wonderful act of remembrance that would be', I thought to myself.

As I was leaving The Great Northern Inn I let Sharon know that I would be coming back in the next day and would bring in some more photos of Steve Bloomer on my laptop to show her. I also suggested to her that she might want to try and get *Steve Bloomer's Watchin'* recorded by Robert Lindsay and the Pride Park Posse on her jukebox for her customers to listen to.

On my drive home back to Pear Tree my mind started to drift away dreaming about things that never were and then thinking to myself, 'Why not?'. What if the city of Derby could erect a statue of Steve Bloomer, just like the town of Middlesbrough had done with Brian Clough in Albert Park. A monument to Steve Bloomer in Pear Tree would be a wonderful thing to see. Back in the heart of the community where he once lived, went to school and played his football. Or maybe they could shift the memorial in the Fish Market to a better location. Sharon had told me that a friend of Steve Richards had phoned her after reading the article in the

Derby Evening Telegraph and mentioned that Steve Bloomer's extended family had never truly been happy with the placement of the memorial in the Fish Market.

It would be a dream come true for me to see another monument to him unveiled in Derby.

There was already one in Cradley, Worcestershire. A memorial to Cradley's Steve Bloomer, the first football superstar, stands in Bridge Street, opposite the row of houses where he was born on Tuesday, 20th January 1874.

On Wednesday, October 24th I returned to The Great Northern Inn having downloaded 11 photos of Steve Bloomer onto my laptop, as well as finding some actual moving footage of Steve Bloomer in his early middle age years, looking quite healthy.

The 1922 footage had been recorded in Liverpool, Merseyside. The video was from the British Pathé archive files 'Steve Bloomer – Famous International footballer, leaves to train Canada's Army Football Team'. In the 35-second clip Steve Bloomer was shown wearing a large flat cap walking around the deck of a ship with officials. It then showed a close up of Steve Bloomer waving and then taking off his hat and waving that in the air.

This was the only moving footage of Steve Bloomer I could find. Unfortunately it had no audio of Steve Bloomer actually speaking. It was my hope to show this video to Steve Richards if he did indeed one day come back to visit The Great Northern Inn pub again.

Sharon had been great, she wanted to honour Steve Bloomer as much as I did and I just knew I had to do my best to help her achieve that. Once again in Steve Bloomer's time of need, another landlady at The Great Northern Inn had taken him in. Just like his beloved daughter Doris had done 70 years previously.

*

On Thursday, October 25th I decided to visit the *Panjab Times* office on Bridle Gate Lane in Derby. It was my hope that they could also share the story from the *Derby Evening Telegraph* article, but this time in Punjabi for their readership. I felt it was a good news story for them to share, about how a British born Punjabi man went searching around Pear Tree for Steve Bloomer; a local legend. At first the reporter I talked to wondered why I wanted to promote such a story. So I explained to him who I was and who my father was and how he had died. I told him that I didn't want them to report how my father died but just to promote the story so that all those who read it would make the connection that I was Mohinder Singh Dhindsa's son. I wanted to show my Punjabi community that the death of my father by suicide was not going to stop me from living my life and sharing the things that most mattered to me.

I guess the taboo of discussing suicide in the Punjabi community, even back, then was something that had always bothered me. I also mentioned to the reporter the name of my big mamma, Avtar Singh Thiara. He then mentioned that my mamma was in a book that he had written himself called 50 Years of Punjabis in Derby. I told the reporter that I had a copy and even though it was written in Punjabi I had managed to read it and recognised many of the faces and profiles within. I then started talking to the reporter about what I hoped to do with my own story. A story about the death of my father and the impact it had on my life. I wanted people to read it so that his memory would never die.

As I was explaining this to the reporter it dawned on me, these guys publish books. If they can do it. Then so can I. All I had to do was finish writing my story. And then once I had done that I could think about publishing it myself too. It was in my hands. No one else was going to write my book for me. I had to write it myself. I had to write it in my own time and on my own terms and in the process of remembering my old neighbourhood I would make sure that my father was never forgotten too.

A few minutes later I was walking back home to Pear Tree, still smiling because of the revelation I just had. As I saw my house on the hill, in the distance I began skipping towards it. Just like days of old as I would make my way home from school to share some good news with my mother.

Chapter 21: Crossed Wires

On Monday, October 29th I received an email from Hasan Patel enquiring if I had made contact with BBC Radio Derby regarding the Steve Bloomer story in the *Derby Evening Telegraph*.

Hasan was an old friend of mine who I first met at the University of Leicester. He graduated in 2001 with a Bachelor of Arts (BA) in History and Politics and then subsequently, a Master of Arts (MA) in International Relations and Affairs in 2003. During this time he was working as a Broadcast Journalist for BBC Radio Leicester. Having been in this job for just over a year he also had hopes to one-day work for the Al Jazeera English News Channel.

I hadn't even thought about contacting Radio Derby. So I let him know that I would get in touch with them immediately by emailing them and including a link to the online article. A few minutes later Hasan sent me another email to inform me that he had been in contact with Radio Derby and that I should expect a call from Katie Townsend very soon. Katie then called me on my mobile. Hasan had already filled her in on the article and the obvious link to Derby suggesting that it would be a good idea to have me on local radio. Katie agreed and then asked me if I could meet her at The Great Northern Inn at half two the following day so that she could interview me.

Unbelievable. I was in the newspaper for the first time ever on Monday, October 22nd then just over a week later I would be on the radio. How was this even possible? After my father's death all I wanted to do was completely shut myself away and never have to deal with the outside world again. But now, well Steve Bloomer had done it again. Once again he had opened up another door for me.

A couple of hours later Sharon called me on my mobile to ask me if I was aware of the radio appointment for the following day. She was just as excited that the Steve Bloomer story would be covered on Radio Derby for all to hear.

On Tuesday, October 30th I made my way to The Great Northern Inn as requested, with my friend Sib once again tagging along.

I decided to arrive early so that it would give me a bit more time to catch up with Sharon. I was also feeling quite anxious and needed to settle my nerves before I would go live on the radio. To distract myself from the worries, I had brought some books along with me and then sat at a table flicking through them as Sib ordered some drinks. As we sat down and took sips from our drinks I began to think to myself, 'what if Katie asks why I went searching for Steve Bloomer in the first place? What if I tell her it was connected to my father? What if she asks me about my father? Would I be able to tell her? Suicide? What was I even doing here?'.

I was just not used to being happy and it was almost as if my body was telling me that I was doing something wrong and that I shouldn't be there. As the minutes ticked on neither Katie or Sharon had appeared and I began to get even more anxious. It was now half two and Sib had gone off to play some pool with one of the regulars.

I sat at the table alone, head down and deep in thought when the jukebox suddenly spluttered into life and began playing a song that I immediately recognised. I lifted my head and smiled. It was the song *JCB* by the folk band Nizlopi. As I listened to the lyrics, they took me back to my own childhood and memories of my own father. I drifted back to the days when my father was also a giant standing beside me. Sitting in his toolbox as he fixed things around the house. The journeys to and from school. Searching for Transformers in toyshops all over Derby. Slouching on the couch watching B.A Baracus and the A-Team. Trying to stay up late at night hoping to catch a Bruce Lee film as I waited for my father to come back home from work. It was all coming back to me. The sadness disappeared as I remembered the many times my father and I also had a top laugh.

Sharon had now arrived and began showing Sib and I some new signs that she had made as well as pictures of Steve Bloomer she had acquired for the pub. Sharon then passed me an open envelope with a letter inside that she had recently received. 'It's from Steve Richards. Have a read' she said, smiling.

I took the letter from her and then began to read it, almost in disbelief, as it slowly began to dawn on me that it was written by Steve Bloomer's grandson. I could not believe it. Steve Richards had thanked Sharon for the article in the paper and then on top of that he thanked me too for what I had done. He had even referred to me by my full name. I had done it. After all these years, I had managed to make contact with Steve Bloomer's family and they had personally thanked me for not forgetting him. Steve Richards also mentioned that his family in South Africa had also seen the article in the *Derby Evening Telegraph* and that they felt very proud and honoured to see it in the newspaper. The letter also revealed that many of Steve Bloomer's souvenirs and memorabilia that were originally passed down to his family after his death had also unfortunately been sold to pay for the memorial in the Lock-Up Yard as well as other things. 'How very sad', I thought to myself.

A few minutes later Katie arrived and then began setting up for the live interview with Sharon and myself. The interview itself did not last very long and mostly covered what was in the newspaper article. I was happy with that and answered all the questions put to me to the best of my ability whilst excitedly informing the listeners of what an absolute hero Steve Bloomer was to me.

A funny thing then happened at the end of the interview when Katie passed back to Alex Trelinski in the studio. As I still had the BBC earphones on I heard him tell the listeners that I was the son of the late Mayor of Derby, Nirmal Singh

Dhindsa. This had me in stitches. Sharon saw me laughing and asked what he had said. So I explained the mistake to her. 'Did that upset you?', she asked. 'No, it didn't', I replied with a smile.

I emailed Alex later in the day to let him know of his mistake and he apologised, but it didn't matter. The whole point of me opening myself up to the media was to make sure my father was not forgotten. Therefore I found it quite funny that he had now been propelled to the late Mayor of Derby.

After leaving The Great Northern Inn and then dropping Sib off at his home I paid another visit to the offices of the *Panjab Times*. I informed them of my earlier appearance on Radio Derby. They then asked me a few more questions about the story they were going to print about Steve Bloomer. They also asked me to send them some pictures of Steve Bloomer and myself.

The next day on Wednesday, October 31st I decided to spend some time in the new house on Breedon Avenue. Rav and I hadn't moved in yet and were still carrying out some home improvements. I had to be there to wait for some deliveries, so I busied myself until the deliveries arrived. It was a good distraction because I knew that today would also be the day that the Steve Bloomer story would also be published in the *Panjab Times*. After a few hours of waiting around the deliveries finally arrived and I had also managed to get a few little things done in the house. Afterwards I decided to drive back home towards Pear Tree and then head towards the *Panjab Times* office to see if the latest edition of the newspaper had been printed. On arrival at the *Panjab Times* I was told that the story had been published, so I thanked them and bought two copies. I drove home to show my mother.

I walked into the living room, sat down on the sofa and began to flick through the pages of the newspaper until I found the story. It didn't take long, as the same pictures that were used in the *Derby Evening Telegraph* were also used in the *Panjab Times*. There he was again, Steve Bloomer alongside Sharon and myself. I let out a laugh then called out for my mother. I began to read what had been published in Punjabi whilst also translating it into English in my mind at the same time. 'Kalwinder Singh Dhindsa of Portland Street, Derby is keeping the memory of Steve Bloomer alive', the headline read. It then went on to repeat some of the information in the *Derby Evening Telegraph* article as well as mentioning his playing days for the Rams. Although the little write up didn't mention my father, anyone reading the story in my local Punjabi community would have known immediately that I would have been the son of Mohinder Singh Dhindsa of Portland Street. They would also have seen a picture of me smiling back at them. That made me feel good because it would show the readers that I was still proud of my old neighbourhood. Just like my father had always been.

My mother then entered the living room so I showed her the newspaper for her to read. She began smiling and seemed quite excited in knowing that many more people would read it too. A few minutes later the phone rang and it was my big mamma calling to let my mother know that I was in the *Panjab Times*. So she told him that she already knew because I was sitting in the living room now having already bought two copies.

What a month it had been. My world seemed to have been turned upside down for the better. I couldn't thank Steve Bloomer enough. He seemed to be showing me the way. Where? I didn't know, but I was certainly heading in the right direction it seemed. I was happier than I had ever been in a long while.

In early November I managed to print an 18" x 12" photo of Steve Bloomer. Thankfully a member of staff at Derby County F.C. was able to provide me with a digital copy after I'd told them what I intended to use it for. I donated this photo of Steve Bloomer to The Great Northern Inn. Sharon was very pleased with the photo and said that she would make sure she displayed it on the wall as soon as possible, in a suitable frame. What pleased me more than anything about this photo was that it was the same picture as the one used on the front cover of Peter Seddon's Steve Bloomer biography.

W. W. Winter Ltd is still Derby's longest established family photography studio and has been on Midland Road since 1852. This original photo of Steve Bloomer was taken in their studio during the early twentieth century.

On Wednesday, November 7th I received a call from Sharon telling me that Steve Richards had been back in touch with her. She hadn't heard anything from him since the letter he'd sent to us. Sharon then informed me that he was now out of hospital and in much better health after having a pacemaker installed. Sharon also mentioned that Steve Richards had also asked for my mobile number and wanted to get in touch with me personally.

It seemed more than likely now that I would one day get to meet Steve Bloomer's grandson. What a great honour that would be for me to tell Steve Richards how much I admired his grandfather and how much Steve Bloomer had helped me in my quest for happiness. I could also tell him about my desire to write and one day release a book too.

I now truly believed that I was onto something and that Steve Bloomer would play a big part in whatever it was. But would meeting Steve Richards be enough to turn the tide of my heartache at losing my father? Would my road to happiness also end there? What would I do after that? As happy as I was with all the good news and things that were occurring off the back of the original Steve Bloomer article in the *Derby Evening Telegraph*, I also knew full well that this level of happiness could not be sustained and sooner or later I could fall and crash again. My spirits could not be sustained surely? I had no idea what lay for me in the future but I did know that the journey I was on now was the start of the beginning to something better. I just knew it. Deep down inside I felt that some good would come out of all this. All I had to do was just keep going with it and not give up. It was the only way to keep moving forward. I had achieved such a great deal in the last month; good news after good news. I was the son of Mohinder Singh Dhindsa the people would say. I was making something positive come out of his death. His suicide, yet I was still reluctant to talk about how my father died.

A few days later on Tuesday, November 13th I received an email from Gemma Hosking from Supply Desk. She informed me that she had found me some work at Hind Leys Community College in Shepshed. This particular school was right next door to Shepshed High School where I had taught a couple of years previously during my PGCE training course with the University of Leicester. It would be my first teaching placement since I had walked away from John Port School. I would be going into Hind Leys Community College on Tuesday, 20th November for the first time.

However, before my return to Shepshed, on Friday, 16th November I sat my Approved Driving Instructor (ADI) Theory Test. There were two parts to the test: multiple-choice questions and hazard perception. Having spent the last few weeks going through every question on the database I managed to achieve a 100% score for both parts and pass the test with flying colours.

When I first told Rav I wanted to leave John Port School, I needed to have a back up plan; I had all but had enough of teaching. This change in career that I looked into was to train to become a driving instructor. The 'golden hello' money I received from passing my NQT was spent on this course.

I had originally signed up with a Driving School with great enthusiasm to try something different and possibly set myself up for another future career too. However, having got a third of the way through the course I realised it was not for me. I had once again blitzed my way through the theory tests by achieving a score of 100% but in the end I just didn't want to see it through. The practical side of it and sitting in the passenger seat whilst trying to instruct others how to drive began to fill me with great anxiety. Once again I felt I didn't have absolute control in my life. It was a case of jumping out of the frying pan and into the fire. Control is what I needed most back in my life and I really needed to be behind my own life's steering wheel.

I had tried it and I had found that I was not comfortable with it. I did lose a bit of money having paid for the course but I had to put my happiness first from now on. It was a life experience I accepted and then quickly moved on from. In the end I think I realised that I was better off sticking to what I knew. Just because I had a not so good experience at John Port School didn't mean that all other schools would be the same.

On reflection at the time I had realised that I was out of John Port School and that was the main thing for me. But I did wonder whether the driving course was just an excuse to get out of my predicament. Were things really that bad in my life at the time for me to plan such an escape?

I finally decided to terminate the driving instructor course in late 2008. It had shown me the pitfalls of trying but failing to succeed. It was another hiccup in my life and I knew that life still had many more disappointments to come. But even after experiences like this I should not give up on trying all things I want to pursue.

Life was never going to be a bed of roses after my father's death. But I also knew that there would be good times. They might be few and far between, but they would come. I had to hope. There was always hope. Hard work would pay off. Dreams could come true. Bad times would not last. I had to grasp all the opportunities that fell at my feet and pursue them determinedly when they did come. Steve Bloomer would guide me along the way, I was sure of it.

Chapter 22: For The Bairns

On Tuesday, November 20th I returned to the town of Shepshed for the first time since my PGCE teacher training days to report to work at Hind Leys Community College. It was also the first time I had set foot in a classroom again as a teacher since I left John Port School the previous year. On that morning I made sure to set off quite early so that I could arrive in Shepshed and meet the cover supervisor by 8:30. The journey from Derby to Shepshed was not a great distance but the traffic on route did result in the journey taking much longer than I expected. As usual I went on an empty stomach, apart from my solitary cup of tea. On arrival, I was taken into the staffroom and by great coincidence I bumped into a former colleague from John Port School, Angie. It was great to see her again. A few minutes later I was taken into a classroom to cover a registration and as soon as I stepped foot into the room a young girl shouted out, 'Mr Dhindsa!' in great excitement. I hadn't even introduced myself to the class, so I looked up to see who had called out my name. I recognised the face of the young student and as I observed the faces of others around her I realised that I recognised many more too. They were former students from my days at Shepshed High School, the school across the road. They were now a couple of years older, but they still remembered me. After all my anxieties about fitting in as an outsider, being in the company of these students made me feel more at ease. It was good to see all their faces again. Later in the afternoon, on my return home to Pear Tree, I emailed Gemma to let her know that I would like to go back to the school because having a bond with some of the students might work in my favour, although I also knew that it might become a problem if they became a little too familiar. So I told Gemma that working at Hind Leys for a term would be fine with me just as long as I could see the light at the end of the tunnel, knowing that I would not stay for too long.

About a month later the school invited me back so that the science department could further ascertain my suitability for the position of a short-term cover placement. On that day the headmistress popped into one of the classes I was covering to see how I was getting on with the students. As I knew a few of the children within the class they were all on their best behaviour and seemed to be quite comfortable in my presence. I guess this impressed the school's management. The school therefore decided to take me on for a 12-week period from January to March 2008. Rav was also very pleased that I had found myself some full-time work again.

I returned to Hind Leys at the start of January 2008 to commence my placement. In the beginning it was quite a pleasant experience to be working again. But as the weeks went on I began to once again lose my enthusiasm for the job. I did work with some great students and some very good staff, but after a time the same issues arose again in terms of misbehaviour and a poor attitude towards learning and education. It began to feel like John Port School all over again; banging my head against a brick wall especially with those students in the lesser ability classes who had by now all but given up in their final year of GCSE education.

During this time I also had a mighty scare in relation to my writing. Whenever I would use my laptop to write my story I would always make sure to save my progress on a USB stick. I would also use this same USB stick to save all my school files. On one particular day I was walking into work carrying my leather satchel in hand. As I made my way into a classroom I looked down at my satchel and noticed my USB stick balancing precariously on the top of a zipped compartment. I couldn't believe it. It had been in my shirt pocket one moment and the next it was down at my feet. My heart sank as I realised just how close I was to losing all that

I had written. I had by now been writing my story for a good few months and I could have lost it all in a split second had my USB fallen straight onto the floor. I was so grateful that day that I had not lost it forever as it would have been very unlikely that someone would have handed it in had they found it. On reflection I thought, 'What if I had lost it that day? Would I have given up on my writing? Would I have been able to start again? Would I even have had the desire to want to start again?'. I had written so much and it had taken so much out of me. Thankfully I didn't lose it and at the end of that day I went home and made sure I backed it all up on my PC too.

There were some good times in Hind Leys, though. Especially when the subject of football would crop up. The children from Shepshed, tended to either support Derby County F.C., Leicester City F.C. or Nottingham Forest F.C. The majority of them either supported Derby or Leicester though due to the closer proximity of the two cities to Shepshed. I personally liked the Rams connection especially considering that Shepshed was once known as Sheepshead or Sheepshed during it's early history when the village was heavily involved in the wool industry.

Towards the middle of February I signed up to an online Derby County Fans Forum, which was hosted by the *Derby Evening Telegraph*. My username was Pear Tree Ram or PTR for short and not long after joining I noticed a petition that had been created by a young Rams fan called Ashley Wilkinson. Ashley had heard about Nottingham's plans to erect a statue to Brian Clough and wanted Derby to also do something similar. As soon as I came across this petition I immediately wanted to lend my support to Ashley so, without any hesitation I also added my name to the growing number of signatures. I then made contact with Ashley through Facebook as I knew that I could get the *Derby Evening Telegraph* behind this campaign too. I also set up a Facebook group to promote the campaign. Within a very short period of time, Claire Duffin of the *Derby Evening Telegraph* then published an article on Thursday, February 21st with the headline 'We want Cloughie here!'. Ashley and I were also shown pictured together outside Pride Park, having had our photo taken the day before the article was published.

WE WANT CLOUGHIE HERE!

Thursday, February 21st 2008 – The Derby Telegraph
By Claire Duffin.

A Campaign has been launched calling for a life-size statue of Brian Clough at Pride Park stadium.

Teenage Rams fan Ashley Wilkinson has set up an online petition through social networking website Facebook to put pressure on Adam Pearson, Derby's chairman of football operations, to commission a statue of the former manager.

More than 50 people have joined the group, and 167 fans have signed up to the petition started by the Littleover Community School pupil.

The club has already unveiled plans for a permanent memorial in some form to Mr Clough, but not necessarily a statue, as part of the Pride Plaza scheme - a £20m development including shops and bars at Pride Park.

"Cloughie put Derby on the map," said season ticket holder Ashley, 17, of Springdale Court, Mickleover.

"While the Pride Plaza gesture is appreciated, the aim of this petition is to make plans for a large statue of Clough to stand

outside the stadium."

Teacher Kalwinder Singh Dhindsa also helped set up the Facebook group, and has posted pictures, videos and information on the site.

"Brian Clough is my hero and it's about time the people of Derby had something fitting to recognise him," said Mr Dhindsa, of Portland Street.

Under the Pride Plaza scheme, a square is to be named after Mr Clough, and the club said it would be erecting a small monument to him and Rams striking legend Steve Bloomer, but was still in discussions over details.

The online group's creator, Billy Gwinnutt, said he felt compelled to act after seeing a large Clough statue was to be built in Nottingham's Market Square and wanted something similar in Derby.

"Now the club has new owners who want to improve the Derby County experience, it seems an obvious way of doing it," he added.

The club is in discussions with Mr Clough's family over the Plaza monument.

Unbelievably, within no time at all a Brian Clough Statue Campaign had been kicked off and the ball was well and truly rolling as the number of signatures increased rapidly.

However, even at this very early stage of the campaign, I had one slight reservation about the end goal. As much as I wanted to see a statue of Brian Clough in Derby, deep down I desperately wanted to see Peter Taylor stand shoulder to shoulder with Brian Clough. I had even discussed changing the petition proposal with Ashley in the hope that I could push this change through. But as much as I tried it seemed that the general consensus of Rams fans was that Brian Clough was enough therefore there was no need to change the petition. At the time Ashley agreed with the consensus. It saddened me a great deal. I was well aware of Peter Taylor's contribution to the success of the Clough and Taylor partnership but other fans around me obviously didn't feel the same way. Although, there were a few that also asked for the inclusion of Peter Taylor too. It was a great shame that Peter Thomas Taylor had almost become a forgotten hero. He deserved much better.

The day after the article was published in the *Derby Evening Telegraph*, news of my appearance in the newspaper had gone around school and there was great excitement from fellow Rams fans who wanted to know more about the campaign. One of my students had family in Derby and had stumbled across me in the paper and then let it be known to all her friends and family that I was in the paper. I also showed a few of them the link to the online article when they asked about the campaign during lesson time.

Whilst at Hind Leys I also ended up working alongside another old friend, Gilly, from my Village Community School days. I had referred him to Supply Desk. Towards the end of February I knew that my time working at Hind Leys was drawing to an end. I was originally supposed to work up until Thursday, March 20th but that just seemed too far away in the distance for me at the time. Another big day in March that was also fast approaching was Saturday, March 1st 2008, the day that would mark the second anniversary of my father's passing.

The day before March 1st would usually be February 28th. However, 2008 was a leap year so Friday, February 29th became a leap day. Therefore, I was technically at school on the two-year anniversary of my father's death.

On this particular day I was working at Hind Leys but in the back of my mind all I kept reflecting on throughout the day was how much my life had changed since the first anniversary of my father's death. I was now definitely in a better place with all the things I was engaged in that made me happy, but the anxieties and the upset in relation to my father's suicide still remained within. Another anniversary day had come again and I had to live through all the heartache and the bad memories all over again. And this would continue to occur for every year of my life thereafter. This day would always be a sad and somber day for me. There was unlikely to ever be any joy in my life on this day. There would only be sadness. March 1st would always be the day my father died. The day of death; D Day. Even though today I would be remembering all that on February 29th.

That afternoon I returned home to Pear Tree and then sat silently in front of my PC. It was switched on but I wasn't in the right frame of mind to engage with it. So I just sat at my chair with my elbows resting on the desk and my face in my hands. It had been a strange day with it also being a leap day and my mind was a jumble of thoughts. 'Two years ago today my father died. No. Two years ago tomorrow my father died?', I kept thinking to myself.

Suddenly my thoughts were distracted by the sound of the back door opening and closing. A second or so later Rav then called out, 'I'm home' as she then rushed through the kitchen and then up the stairs. I remained where I was not being able to move a muscle. A minute or so later Rav then called out in excitement and asked me to join her upstairs in the bathroom. A little bit of worry now consumed my thoughts so I quickly made my way up the stairs to check up on her. I entered the bathroom, a little puzzled as to what she may have wanted to tell me so urgently. I observed her face; it looked a little flushed and somewhat glowing. 'You ok?', I asked. 'Yep' she replied smiling. 'What's up?', I asked. Rav then thrust what looked like a marker pen into my face. 'Look at this!', she laughed. I looked on in confusion. 'Aren't you going to say anything?', she asked, quite confused. It took a second or so for the penny to drop. 'We're going to have a baby', she then said. 'Show me', I asked in disbelief. As I looked at the pregnancy test I saw the positive test result to confirm that she was indeed pregnant. I was dumbstruck. I just walked out and then went back downstairs and returned to my PC to once again sit looking at the wall but this time with my mouth wide open trying to assimilate what had just happened. Rav then entered the room and approached me. She could see how stupefied I was to hear the news. I still couldn't believe what had just happened as I looked up and smiled at her. I then gave her a hug and laughed. We were going to have a baby. I was going to become a father. I was over the moon as a warm fuzzy feeling of great happiness washed over me.

Two years to the day my father had passed away I had found out that Rav and I were going to have a baby. It was indeed the happiest day of my life.

On Wednesday, March 12th I worked my last day at Hind Leys. Eight days short of the 20th when I was initially supposed to finish. In the end I had no choice but to finish early. My health was also beginning to suffer as I was constantly feeling exhausted. The long trips into work and sometimes arriving late having got stuck in heavy traffic was becoming a bit too much to. It would give me no time to relax nor do any preparation if required before my first lesson even began.

Enough was enough. Once again I knew I was in trouble when I began counting down the days to the finish, just like all those years previously at Toyota in Burnaston. As another teacher at school who was a bit older than me would say to me, 'You don't want to wish your life away counting down the days'. He was right I didn't want to wish my life away, but there was another reason I was also counting the days. I wanted to be at home close to Rav preparing for the baby as well as our house move. We would be parents by the end of the year. I would be a father provided everything went well and the baby was born in good health.

On my last day at Hind Leys I was thanked by the science department for all my efforts and was kindly given a black Parker pen as a leaving present, which was very nice of them. I had tried my best but my anxieties were once again getting the better of me. When all was said and done it really was nice to see some old faces again, but as the weeks went on the same issues I had at John Port School arose at Hind Leys too. The main one being that I was not able to do my job as a teacher to the best of my ability due to misbehaviour in the classroom and lack of interest shown by some students towards their education. I was also having issues with my disposition. Going from extreme highs to intense lows were completely knocking me out of my rhythm. A further source of anxiety was the constant thought that I had a story to write up but I wasn't able to tell my story as I wanted to. Nor did I have any idea as to where my story was going and what the end point would be if ever there was one at all. The revelation that Rav and I were expecting our first child also hastened my decision to leave and further added to my anxieties and worries for the future ahead. My mood was all over the place.

But one thing I did know was that I needed to remain happy and positive. Knowing that I would finish a week or so earlier than I intended to I decided to use those days I now had free to move the rest of our possessions from our Pear Tree home into the Breedon Avenue home. I could also begin painting and assembling things ready for Rav and myself to move in April, before my sister's wedding. There would be a baby on the way and we needed to be ready for the big move, but we weren't going to tell anyone until Rav's first scan at 12 weeks.

On the day I retuned home to Pear Tree having working my last day at Hind Leys Community College I was comfortably sat on the sofa flicking through the channels of my TV when

I caught sight of a familiar logo on screen. The BBC East Midlands Today programme was showing a news piece about my old University. As I turned the volume up I heard a story about a man called Tim Grigg who worked at the University of Leicester. In this piece Tim revealed that on Wednesday, December 5th 2007 he had received a phone call from his step-mum informing him that his father had gone missing. On hearing this news, he realised the seriousness of the situation so immediately jumped into his car and drove 180 miles to help find his father. On arrival he joined in the search to try and find his father. Unfortunately, on Friday, December 7th 2007 his father was found. Tim's father had decided to end his life in a forest near his home.

I continued to listen on as my eyes glazed over thinking about my own father and how he had also died by his own hands. My father had decided to end his life in exactly the same way as Tim's father but I wasn't talking to people about how he died. Yet here was Tim Grigg on the TV talking so bravely about his father's death and sharing it with the world. 'What an amazing act of bravery; that took some courage', I thought to myself.

Tim went on to reveal that the death of his father had come as a great shock to all his family, as it was so sudden and without explanation. He then also shared the torment that he had gone through in his life since the death of his father and the many questions that had played through his mind since; the need to try and understand what had driven his father to do such a thing. I could totally relate to this as I had been living the same torment in my own life.

Tim then went on to say that he had talked to others who had also been in this horrible situation and only then did he begin to realise just how common suicide and depression was. How closely they are linked together to each other, and how misunderstood it is by many. At the end of the news piece Tim said he wanted the public's help to raise money for the Charlie Waller Memorial Trust and try and help promote the importance of having a better awareness of the well-being of our families, friends and work colleagues; to raise awareness of the nature and dangers of depression.

On Saturday, June 14th 2008 Tim would begin The Long Journey Home. He would aim to run 180 miles in 7 days, carrying 30lbs of weight. Starting the run from Enderby,

Leicester and finishing in Carnforth town on the Lancashire / Cumbrian border.

Tim's father had been struggling with his mental health just like my own father. They were both deeply depressed, but just didn't have anyone to turn to, to ask for help.

When the news piece finally finished I switched the TV off and reflected on what I had just seen and heard. That's it. That's what it was all about. To make something positive come out of something so bad.

On hearing Tim's story I immediately tracked him down on Facebook within a few minutes and then made a donation to the charity he was raising funds for. I also let him know about my father's own death by suicide and how seeing him on TV talking about his father's death made me also want to try and make a difference one day too.

I could totally understand what Tim was trying to do. I had been reflecting constantly on the same thoughts ever since my father had passed away. Yet initially I was far too reluctant to even try to open myself up. But in recent months I had begun to emerge more and more out of my shell. Even though I would still think of myself as a shy person, in recent times I had begun to regularly appear in the local media. I was opening up and deep down I knew I was doing it primarily so that people would associate me with my father when they saw me. In that way they too would remember him, but so far, I had not mentioned at all how my father had died.

Tim Grigg had reinforced to me that when people take their lives in such a manner, it is all too easy for others to forget about them and not talk about them any more. But no good person should ever be forgotten in death. From that moment on I just knew that all I ever wanted to do in my life from now on was to get off my backside and do something that would make a difference, to hopefully change people's lives as well as my own by promoting mental health awareness and sharing my father's story.

Another good piece of fortune also helped cement my desire to promote mental health awareness especially in my own community. One day, I visited Waterstones in Derby with my friend Sib. As we entered the store I noticed a strangely familiar face on one of the bookshelves. The face looked like a younger version of myself but in fact the boy with the topknot staring straight back at me was a young British-born Punjabi author from Wolverhampton called Sathnam Sanghera. The book he had recently released was called 'If you don't know me by now – A memoir of love, secrets and lies in Wolverhampton'. As I moved in closer to the display I picked the book off the shelf and began reading the blurb. This particular book also seemed to be about a father and son relationship.

In time I would read Sathnam's memoir and realise that by just seeing the image of that little Sikh boy and his topknot on the front cover that day was all the impetus I required to eventually release my own book about my father too.

The month of April was a difficult period in my life. Not only did it bring the day Rav and I finally moved out of Pear Tree to our new home in Blagreaves. But it also brought the day of my sister's wedding. Over the last few weeks Rav and I had been progressively working on our new house in preparation to completely move out of Pear Tree by Friday, April 4th, one day before my sister's wedding.

My sister's wedding hadn't been a happy occasion for me. For the previous few months I had tried my utmost best to remain in high spirits by keeping myself busy. Steve Bloomer and Brian Clough had made sure of that. My constant desire to remember the past resulted in many occasions where I would try to share what I was doing with others. Most of the people I would engage with would be happy to listen and talk. However, sometimes I would come across people who just didn't want to know. On one occasion I excitedly tried to get someone's attention by trying to show them something that I was deeply interested in, but this person immediately snapped back at me telling me that they didn't care one bit for what I was doing. This really hurt me, because there was a legitimate reason as to why I was trying to engage with people. I was trying to make links to my past. By sharing where I came from and who I was. To help me remember my father and maybe allow others to speak about him in conversation too. To make others understand too. But some people obviously did not share the same sentiment and I had to quickly accept that some people just don't think like me. They just don't think. From that moment on I just stopped talking to these people. I just couldn't have people like them in my life. Joy sappers who would deflate my happiness. On the day of my sister's wedding I was totally detached from it all. I hardly involved myself with anything and I didn't really engage with anyone. I was completely out of the loop.

I was missing my father terribly. He should have been at the wedding to give my sister away himself. I've never liked weddings and big occasions. I've always found them too busy and loud. And for someone like me it was the worst place to engage with people; a crowded room was indeed the loneliest place. It was no place to talk with people on a one-to-one basis. There were far too many people to speak to and I wanted to speak to them all individually, but as I couldn't and didn't want to leave anyone out. I ended up trying not to speak to anyone. I was painting myself into a corner but all I could think about was trying to remain on my own road to happiness. I couldn't allow others to knock me off my path. My whole life depended on it. I couldn't afford to take my eye off the ball and follow in the same tragic footsteps as my father before me.

After 28 years of living in Pear Tree I had now moved out. Yes, it did upset me. But as I told my mother, 'It would always be my childhood home'. Nobody could ever take that away from me. It was the link to my past, and my family that would never be broken no matter how far I travelled. I would always come back home when the call came, as I knew my mother would be waiting for me.

The next couple of months brought more anxiety-filled weeks peppered by occasions of happiness and downright surreality. Rav and I had a baby on the way and we had just moved into our new house on Breedon Avenue. I also needed to get back into work but yet didn't want to teach. So I took some more time off to clear my head and get my house in order as well as prepare for the year ahead by pursuing the driving instructor course by working on the practical side of it. Taking the job at Hind Leys for a three-month contract had taken quite a bit out of me and knocked my confidence again. From this point on I knew that I would require shorter placements. So I asked my agency to find me something from July onwards.

On Monday, May 19th Rav and I visited the midwife at Lister House Surgery on Harrington Street to check upon the health of the new baby. We had been waiting in anticipation for this for a while now since we first began seeing the midwife. Thankfully all was fine and as soon as the scanner detected the baby's heartbeat my nerves settled down although my heart skipped many beats in anticipation of hearing a heartbeat. To my relief it sounded like a galloping horse.

As Rav and I were leaving the surgery I decided to make an appointment with a GP to discuss my concerns with my own mental health. I had discussed it with Rav beforehand and felt that now was the right time to discuss my mental state with a medical professional. The appointment with the GP was scheduled for the very next day at 9:30am.

On Tuesday, May 20th I arrived at the surgery quite early, registered that I had arrived and then waited for my turn to be seen by the GP. As I sat there waiting I realised that my father would have sat waiting in the exact position as me many a time a couple of years previously for exactly the same reason. Before I could think any more of it, my name was called, and I was asked to make my way to see the GP.

When I reached his room I knocked on the door and then waited to be called inside. On entry the GP greeted me and then asked me to explain to him why I wanted to see him. So I began to tell him that I thought I might have some form of manic depression. As I rambled on, he began typing things into his PC and every now and again he would stop and look up to ask another question. As he was doing this I told him all about the highs and lows that I had experienced over the years and some of the most recent ones over the last two years since the death of my father. It was only when I mentioned to him that my father had taken his own life by suicide did he stop typing and then began to listen even more attentively.

Having asked some further questions he told me that I may have a form of depression, but he doubted whether it was manic depression as the people who really did have it tended not to be aware of it. This disappointed me a bit because I had gone in to see him having looked up manic depression on the Internet. I read about manic depression and the milder form of it called Dysthymia and the more I read the more I recognised some of the symptoms that I believed I had also been experiencing. I honestly believed that at times I felt like two people, someone who could he happy and on a high at one time then on other occasions, sad and on a low. To be told I may have had a condition would have been something that I was quite willing to accept. A diagnosis could explain a lot of my anxieties away. Then again on reflection I realised that depression carried too much of a stigma, especially in terms of the way my father lost his life. So maybe it was a good thing that I didn't have it.

The GP then suggested that because I had done some research into Bipolar Disorder, Manic Depression, Hypomania and Dysthymia then I could have also inadvertently tricked myself into thinking that I may have any one of these conditions. This was a fair point, but I was quite sure that I had many of the characteristics associated with the conditions even before I had read into them all.

Towards the end of the appointment I made it clear to the GP that I wanted to see him to find out why I was behaving the way I was. I just wanted to understand the reasons for my behaviour and had not come in for any medicine. I then went on to tell him that I didn't want my condition, whatever it was, to affect the relationship I would have with the newborn baby that Rav and I were expecting in late October. The GP suggested that I talk to a specialist that he knew, a mental health therapist by the name of Chris Roome. I said that was fine by me and he told me that he would pass my details on to the mental health therapist and that he would be in touch with me very soon.

I was hoping that my next visit to the surgery would give me a better idea as to what exactly I have or didn't have. One way or the other, it would give me the kick up the backside I need so that I could get on with the things in my life that I really needed to get completed, i.e. completing my story and also most importantly getting some more supply work so that I could make some more money. As Brian Clough once said, 'Pay off your mortgage as soon as you can. The banks rob you blind'.

On Friday, May 23rd I received a letter in the post from Lister House Surgery. After Tuesday's visit to the surgery my GP had arranged an appointment for me to see the mental health therapist for Tuesday, June 3rd; I immediately texted Chris Roome to confirm that I would be attending.

A week before this appointment Rav and I had made our way up north to see her parents. As we were going to stay over for a few days I decided to take some books along with me to read. Over the course of this trip I managed to read two books and was in the process of reading a third before we returned to Derby.

All three books were essentially about Brian Clough, the first was called *Provided you don't kiss me* by Duncan Hamilton, the second, *Right place, right time* by George Edwards and the third book which I was reading for the second time, was called *The Damned United* by David Peace.

The first time I read *The Damned United*, I really enjoyed it because of the obvious connections to Derby and Derby County F.C. To have my hometown and local football club at the core of a story was great. As a Rams fan it was really easy to get caught up in the euphoria of the Clough and Taylor dream team. But after reading it the first time, I could totally understand why Brian Clough's family would have serious reservations about it.

Normally I didn't read books for a second time after I have read them already, but *The Damned United* was an exception. Around this time, I found out that the BBC were developing the book into a film and there had also recently been an article in the *Derby Evening Telegraph* about the film company asking for extras to attend Saltergate Recreation Ground the home of Chesterfield F.C. These extras would appear as football fans in the crowd for the Baseball Ground scenes as well as other football stadiums they were trying to replicate. I really had high hopes for the film and wanted it to be a success, so I was not going to miss the opportunity of being a part of it, after all, I might even get to meet my great heroes; Clough and Taylor. My old Mackworth College friend Marcus Shukla and I were both big Brian Clough fans so we jumped at the chance to be involved. We were originally told that they needed us for filming on a Tuesday but then we both received a text saying that the filming dates had been changed due to the bad weather so they would get back to us as soon as possible with another date. That date then became Tuesday, June 3rd.

During my time up north I visited the home of Middlesbrough F.C. at the Riverside Stadium with Rav's two brothers. On the way to the stadium we drove past the old location of 34 Parliament Street, the house that Steve Bloomer lived in during his time playing for Middlesbrough F.C.

My reason for wanting to visit the Riverside Stadium was not to go and watch a match, but to actually see the stadium instead, which was basically an exact replica of Pride Park in Derby. I also wanted to see the statues of George Hardwick and Wilf Mannion that the club had erected outside the stadium. The club had also installed the original gates from Ayresome Park outside the stadium too. Both Ayrseome Park and the old Baseball Ground in Derby were bulldozed to the ground to make way for housing developments.

Having seen what I wanted to see at the Riverside Stadium, I asked Rav's brothers to take me to Albert Park as I wanted to see the Brian Clough statue that the people of Middlesbrough had commissioned and unveiled a year previously to remember their local born legend. On seeing the statue and taking a few photos with it, we then drove to the other side of Albert Park so that I could see Brian Clough's old childhood home and the green heritage plaque that was attached to it. Rav's brothers were quite happy to take me down there but refused to get out of the car with me when I wanted to take photos outside the house. They obviously had concerns about our safety in relation to locals taking offence at our presence on their streets, but I wasn't worried one bit. I had come all this way and I was not going to leave without taking a photo of Brian Clough's old home on 11 Valley Road, Grove Hill. After I took some pictures, I got back into the car and we then drove a bit further up the road and stopped again so that I could have a photo taken of me standing next to the Valley Road sign near the roundabout.

As we made our way back we passed the old site of Rea's café on the corner of Ayresome Street. Rea's café was the place where Brian Clough first met his wife, Barbara. It was also where Brian Clough, Peter Taylor and other players of Middlesbrough F.C. would meet after training.

I pointed the building out to Rav's brothers and told them that the café once belonged to the family of Chris Rea, the Middlesbrough born rock and blues singer-song writer whose hit songs included Stainsby Girls. They both then informed me that Rav also went to Stainsby School, which then later became Acklam Grange Secondary.

On the drive back to Rav's parents house I thought about the two statues to Hardwick and Mannion at the Riverside and Brian Clough in Albert Park. They were amazing tributes to Middlesbrough F.C.'s local legends.

If only the City of Derby and Derby County F.C. could get their act together and do the same for my own heroes, such as Bloomer and Clough. 'Will it ever happen?', I thought to myself on the drive back. I didn't know, but I knew that when I got back to Derby I was going to increase my efforts to push something through. I may fail, but at least I could say that I'd tried.

Fortunately for me, in relation to Brian Clough, the ball was already well and truly rolling. Since the article about the Brian Clough Statue Campaign in Derby was published in the Derby Evening Telegraph the number of signatures for the petition had rocketed. A couple of months previously I had designed some A6 Brian Clough Statue Campaign flyers. At the bottom of the flyer was a web address that would take you to Ashley's petition online. Rav's brother Bal had kindly printed hundreds of them off for me for free. I then distributed these flyers far and wide. Derby County F.C. even allowed me to slip them into their programmes that were sold on match day. On one occasion Ashley and I went to the Eagle Centre market to drum up more support and hand them out to passing fans. At one point I was in conversation with a couple of fans and I told them that if the Brian Clough statue was given the green light by Derby County F.C. then it was my hope that Peter Taylor could also stand beside Brian Clough too. As soon as I had mentioned Peter Taylor I was laughed at. 'No chance', they told me. I was a little upset by their reaction but I was not put off. I wouldn't give up. 'I would keep trying', I told myself. For Pete's sake, I would not give up on him.

On Tuesday, June 3rd I would meet my mental health therapist for the very first time. However, this day also coincided with filming in Chesterfield for *The Damned United*. Marcus Shukla and I had already done some filming over the previous days, but on this day I would be going there on my own. So, in the morning I travelled to Chesterfield in my car and as soon as the morning session was complete I drove back to Derby for my appointment to see Chris Roome. Throughout the morning I had kept Chris informed via text as to what I was up to as well as letting him know what time I should appear back in Derby. In the end I made it to the appointment on time.

When I met Chris Roome for the first time, he immediately greeted me with a warm smile and a handshake. This instantly put me at ease as he then began asking me how the filming for *The Damned United* had been going. Chris was a Derby man like myself, born and raised in Normanton. He was also a big Derby County F.C. fan and a season ticket holder at Pride Park. Therefore, he had a real interest in the filming of the *The Damned United* as well as talking about all things Derby County F.C. with me. I could not have been matched with a better person to share my worries.

In answer to his first question I explained to him that I was really enjoying myself observing how the film was being put together especially considering my great admiration for both Clough and Taylor and my obvious pleasure in playing a small part in the film. I also mentioned to him that I was fully aware that the book and the film were obviously a work of fact and much fiction that had to be taken with a hefty pinch of salt.

I had never met Brian Clough or Peter Taylor in the flesh so seeing them at Saltergate portrayed by actors was the closest thing I would ever get to actually meeting them for real. Michael Sheen played Brian Clough and Timothy Spall played Peter Taylor. I had always liked Timothy Spall from the days when he used to play the character of Barry Spence Taylor in Auf Wiedersehen, Pet. I also managed to see a few other stars during the filming such as Jim Broadbent who played Sam Longson (Roy Slater from Only Fools and Horses) and Colm Meaney who played Don Revie (Chief Miles O'Brien from Star Trek: The Next Generation and Star Trek: Deep Space Nine). Seeing Michael Sheen as Brian Clough on the set for the first time was quite a breathtaking moment for me.

During this particular conversation I also mentioned to Chris that I was involved in a campaign to erect a statue for Brian Clough in Derby too; I then handed him one of my flyers. Chris took the flyer out of my hand, looked at it then revealed to me that he was in middle of reading *Provided you don't kiss me* by Duncan Hamilton, the same book that I had read in the previous week.

After a couple of minutes of casual chatter Chris then got straight to the point and asked me why I thought I might have some kind of mental condition. So, I then began to rattle on for another couple of minutes explaining to him how my father's suicide had affected me and how I was now trying to write a book about it all to tell his story.

He looked on puzzled and then asked me why I had not talked about my issues with a bereavement counselor before. So I explained to him how difficult it was do so in my culture. The only way I could open up about it all was to write about it myself and in doing so try to understand and somehow come to terms with my father's death by trying to put it all together as if it was some kind of jigsaw puzzle.

As I continued to chat to Chris I then began to recognise how good it felt to be talking to him like this. He was a stranger yet I was telling him everything. And I was not even worried about what he would think or whether he might even judge me. I had kept my feelings locked up for so long and now here I was letting them all flow freely. At this point I then slowed down my talking pace as it dawned on me what I had just realised. It was good to talk, and I had not done enough of it in the last couple of years. I told him I had tried to talk with people in the past but sometimes it was obvious that they didn't want to talk about certain things. Occasionally they didn't even want to talk about the things that made me happy either. So, all I had was my writing and the books that I would read to lift my spirits.

Chris then asked me what things did make me happy. I began telling him that the vast majority of the things that mean so much to me are all essentially connected to my past; memories and places when my father was still alive. And how these good memories of my past and especially Derby filled me with great happiness as all my roads kept leading me back to Pear Tree, Derby. I also mentioned the significance of Steve Bloomer in my life and how he always seemed to be around when I needed him the most for direction and encouragement.

Having asked me so many questions Chris picked up on my behaviour: he saw that my mind was constantly ticking away. 'You think too much don't you?', he asked. He was right. I thought far too much. And then I realised what he was really getting at. Maybe the reason for my highs and lows was the fact that when I really get into something, I pursue it to the absolute max, and then when I do get low, it may not be down to a mental condition but purely down to a lack of energy. So it was not entirely a mood change thing, it was an energy thing. Maybe it was all down to how I eat. Sometimes when I did get caught up in something completely, I would become too busy to eat, and would only finally force myself to eat something when I was starving. What if this was what was getting me down? For a person who thinks so much, surely my brain would also get tired too? It too requires energy to function properly. It was an interesting point to ponder, to try and understand why I was the way I am and what made me the way I am.

Chris then began to ask me about my fears and anxieties, so I told him about:

How I tend not to answer the phone any more and try to avoid talking to people on it at all cost. The thought of picking it up still scares me momentarily because it always reminds me of the time my brother called me at school to let me know that my father had hanged himself.

How I don't like people getting too close to me so that I am able to hear and feel their breath as it always reminds me of when my father breathed his last rasping breaths of life at the Derbyshire Royal Infirmary.

How I've stopped chatting to certain people in my life because they don't have the same interests as me, and how I take it as a personal insult to my father if they appear to not care about something I am deeply involved in.

How everything I do or involve myself in always relates back to my father in some way because I'm trying to keep his memory alive. I am constantly trying to do my utmost to make sure that he is never forgotten, even if it means that I may rub people up the wrong way in the pursuit of happiness.

How more than anything I also worry about my own mental state. What if I succumb to a mental condition too and have to put my own children through what I experienced with my own father.

At this point Chris asked me if I had any children and I told him that Rav, my wife, was pregnant and we were expecting our first child in a few months. That was another reason I had to write because I knew that the day would come when my child would ask me why their grandfather was not around any more. I would have to tell my child that he had passed away. But how would I tell the child how he had died? I didn't have the answer. I still didn't know the answer myself as to how he died or what led him to take his own life. How would I explain that to a child?

I was so glad that I was now talking to Chris and getting this all off my chest because he might also be able to realise that I was obviously afraid that my mood swings could impact on our newborn child. I didn't want my child to suffer as I had done so with my own father. I had by now revealed so much to Chris; things that I had only ever shared with myself in my own writing. I had never really told anyone else, until now. It really was good to talk. I had been an honest person all my life and I would like to think that one-day when the question was asked of me I could tell the truth. But at this moment in time I didn't know the truth or the answer, but writing helped me to ask the questions.

My greatest fear of them all was that one day I would wake up and forget that my father ever existed; that he had never lived. That was my nightmare. What if a mental illness took my memories away from me? For that reason, I knew I had to write things down so that the memories would last forever on paper, if not always within my mind.

Throughout the whole of our conversation, having told Chris about my father and how he had died, I got the impression that Chris seemed to know who my father was. Maybe he had read up on his medical notes. But then again maybe it was Chris that my father had also been seeing as a patient. I would have asked Chris straight out that day but I knew very well that I would have broken down and began to cry if I found out that Chris had been his therapist. I would have tried to ask Chris what state my father was in when he would have met him. I would then have no doubt pictured my father in my mind trying to tell Chris what was wrong with him as he became more and more frustrated with himself and his inability to communicate and express his thoughts to him. Just like the time before his death when he tried to explain to me the aches and pains he was experiencing and the damage it was doing to his mind. I didn't ask Chris that day if my father was also his patient, but I knew that in time I would. Or that Chris would indeed reveal it to me himself.

Chris wrapped up the appointment by telling me that based on what he had heard from me he thought my high and low parameters were a bit wider than what 'normal' people would have. This basically meant that I just had extreme highs and lows. At least I now knew that it wasn't a serious mental condition. Which I guess was somewhat of a relief to both myself and Rav. Chris then arranged for another appointment in two weeks so that he could check up on me and make sure everything was going well. After our little talk I felt very happy having gotten so much off my chest.

On leaving the surgery, I went to see my mother and grandmother on Portland Street. After I had eaten and shared a cup of tea with them I decided to head back to Chesterfield and involve myself in a bit more filming. However, this time I decided to go for a change in outfit and took one of my father's old coats with me, for added effect in the crowd scenes.

*

On Wednesday, June 15th Rav and I visited the City Hospital for the first time to have her 20-week scan. It would also be the first time we got to have a proper look at the developing baby and it was a wonderful feeling to see the child. A week earlier we'd heard the child's heartbeat and now here we were staring in amazement at a picture of a tiny little wriggling child to be. During this scan we could actually find out the sex of the baby. However, prior to the scan we both decided that we didn't want to know and that we would leave it as a surprise. The sex of the baby didn't matter anyway. All that mattered was that the baby was born healthy. By now we had already told people that Rav was expecting. On the day of the 12-week scan we had purchased a photo of the little bloomer to be and I had shared it with all my family and friends on my Facebook profile to reveal to them all that we were expecting our first child.

*

Chris Roome

Mental Health Therapist

First meeting on Tuesday, June 3rd 2008

"Desperately wants to make his father proud"

Chapter 23: Stoked

On the morning of Saturday, June 14th June I awoke to the voice of Robert Lindsay singing Steve Bloomer's Watchin', it was the ringtone on my mobile. Bleary-eyed; I reach out for my mobile to check who was calling me. It was Sharon the landlady from the Great Northern Inn. I hadn't heard from her in a long while, so I immediately answered her call. Sharon excitedly began to tell me that Steve Richards had visited the pub earlier in the day and informed a member of staff that he was in town to talk to the board of directors at Derby County F.C.

The club was now in discussions with Steve Richards about plans to erect a memorial statue to his legendary grandfather in Pride Park to be unveiled in January 2009. I couldn't believe what I was hearing.

After a long period of not hearing anything about Steve Bloomer, suddenly out of nowhere the possibility of a Steve Bloomer memorial had come alive again. What a fantastic effort Steve Richards had put in, having risen from his hospital bed only a few months previously to still come back and pursue the campaign for Derby County F.C. to honour his grandfather. He never gave up; he would not let his beloved grandfather be forgotten.

Tuesday, July 15th 2008, Steve Bloomer, arguably the greatest player in Derby County's history, is inducted into the National Football Museum Hall of Fame. The legendary striker who scored 332 goals for the Rams in 525 games spread over two spells in the 1890s and early 1900s will now be quite rightly be up there where he belongs.

Steve Bloomer, who also scored 28 times in only 23 international games for England, is widely regarded as football's first superstar.

He joins fellow Derby County legend Dave Mackay in the Hall of fame and is one of nine new additions for 2008. Brian Clough was also inducted as a manager in the European Hall of Fame 2008 special awards.

In the summer of 2008 whilst all these great developments about Steve Bloomer began to gradually make themselves become known I was now back at work having found some new positions with Supply Desk. Thankfully, this time around I was not actually teaching but instead offering my support as a teaching assistant working in a school that catered for children with special needs. This was a new experience for me and on the whole an enjoyable one. Alderwasley Hall School in Wirksworth was the school I worked at and it was a real eye opening experience. During this time of employment I also once again managed to work alongside my old school friend, Gilly; covering for staff that were unavailable to come into work for whatever reason. I also carried out some short-term supply work at other schools around Derbyshire during this time too, such as Woodlands School in Allestree, where Brian Clough had sent his young son Nigel Clough as a child.

During this period of time I also continued to see Chris Roome quite regularly. We discussed how I was getting on in life and how preparations were going with the forthcoming arrival of our baby in late October. Chris also decided to put me on a course called Beating the Blues; a computerised cognitive behavioural therapy (CBT) programme for depression and anxiety, recommended by the National Institute of Health and Clinical Excellence (NICE). Unfortunately, this course really didn't appeal to me and I didn't manage to fully engage with it. The act of talking to

Chris, I feel, worked a lot better for me and the visits to see him although sometimes may have been a bit up and down they did help me a great deal to get many things off my chest that I wouldn't have shared with others at the time.

After a visit to see Chris during the summer holidays on Friday, August 29th, I decided to hook up with my friend Sib in town. On that day we met another friend, Randheer who then was able to give us a lift into Nottingham, where he worked at the time. I had always wanted to visit Nottingham Forest F.C.'s City Ground, so Sib and I decided to walk to the stadium from the city centre. It was my hope that once we got there we could see the Brian Clough bust that was installed in the stadium.

It took Sib and I a while to make it all the way down to the City Ground having asked for directions all along the way. But eventually we walked past Notts County F.C.'s Meadow Lane and then a few minutes later arrived at the City Ground. We then headed toward the Brian Clough Stand and noticed an open door so we went in and up a flight of stairs and entered an area called the Brian Clough Suite. From here we could just about see the pitch. We then decided to hover around for a bit until we were able to ask someone if they knew where the Brian Clough bust was located in the stadium, which we found was located on the other side of the ground in the reception area.

After hanging around for a couple more minutes, we were approached by a member of staff who asked us both what we were doing here. So, I explained that we had come all the way from Derby and were hoping to see the Brian Clough bust, as I was a huge fan. After listening he informed us that it was on the other side of the ground. We got talking to him and he told us that he'd worked at the City Ground for the last 20 years or so and he had known Brian Clough very well. Sib and I then told him our names and he told us that his name was Gerry. 'Where are you both from?', he asked. To which we both replied, 'Derby'. 'No, where are your parents from?', he asked again. 'Oh, right, Punjab in North West India', I replied. 'Where are you originally from?' I asked having detected an accent. 'I'm from Venice', he said. 'Oh right, an Italian', I said. 'Venetian!', Gerry replied. I then asked Gerry about the Brian Clough bust again and whether he would allow us to see it. He seemed a bit reluctant at first because he obviously had work to be getting on with. 'We've come all the way from Derby, it would be a shame to come this far and this close and not be able to see it now', I appealed. That must have changed his mind because he then told us to both wait in an executive's box whilst he carried out some duties.

As Sib and I waited for Gerry we were joined by another Forest fan a bit older than us who was wearing dark sunglasses and seemed to have a walking stick in his hand. This fan then began talking to us both and reminiscing about the good old days when his father and himself would watch home games from the opposite terrace which was called the Main stand. This was the time before Clough and Taylor when the club was managed by Johnny Carey. He asked us if we were big Forest fans too. To our surprise, he laughed when I told him that I was actually a big Derby County fan and that Clough and Taylor were also great heroes of mine. 'I'm planning to get a statue of them both erected in Derby you know?', I told him. He then asked what we were doing here and I explained that we had come in to try and get a glimpse of the Brian Clough bust and that one of the members of staff had told us to wait here inside the executive box until he was free to show us around. He smiled, 'It's so good to be back here again', he said as he began observing all the corners of the ground. As Sib and I also took a good look around I noticed the man raising his hand and then wiping a tear away from his cheek. He was quite obviously overcome by memories of the past. After a couple more minutes Gerry then returned and said he was now free to take us over to reception. We bid the Forest fan goodbye and told him how nice it was talking to him. 'Follow me boys', said Gerry as he led Sib and I around to the other side of the stadium, through the players car park and into the main reception where the Brian Clough bust was located.

As Gerry talked to the receptionist Sib then took some photos of me standing next to the Brian Clough bust and smiling. I actually had my Derby County F.C. jersey on under my hoodie but I decided against showing it off inside the stadium. I didn't want to offend anyone at the club as they had showed such kindness when engaging with me. Gerry then asked Sib and I if we wanted to see the trophy room. 'Is the European Cup inside there?', I asked. 'Yep, sure it is', Gerry replied. Gerry then led Sib and I into the Trophy room and left us in there, alone, for a good five minutes as I took photos and carefully observed all the silverware and pictures on the wall. When Gerry returned we thanked him for being so nice and friendly to us and also trusting us to behave ourselves within the trophy room. We then said goodbye to Gerry and headed out of reception and into the club shop where I purchased a photo of Brian Clough and Peter Taylor with the European Cup, a Brian Clough quote book and a Brian Clough postcard.

A couple of weeks later I was called by a reporter from the *Derby Evening Telegraph* asking me about my opinions on Councilor Joe Naitta's backing for a Brian Clough statue in Derby. Joe Naitta had recently become a Councillor for the Blagreaves ward and obtained the position of Cabinet member for leisure and cultural services in Derby. He had also already visited me at my new house a month previously wanting to talk about the campaign, as he knew that I was involved in it.

At the start of September 2008, Rav and I began intensifying our preparations for the imminent birth of our first child. Over the last few months we had gradually begun to accumulate all the necessities that a newborn child required. One of the most expensive things we purchased was an apple green pushchair. I also began reading the book, *The Bloke's Guide to Pregnancy* by Jon Smith and I found it to be a very good read that prepared me well for the big day ahead.

During these weeks I'd also continued seeing Chris Roome and talked to him about the stresses and anxieties that I still held on to in my life. One major cause of worry was whether I should continue to pursue the driving instructor course? It was now really beginning to stress me out and the constant reminder to get it completed as soon as possible was really beginning to get me down. My heart was just not in it by now. To carry on would have resulted in a very negative effect on my life and no doubt, would not have helped with the upcoming arrival of the newborn child. I wanted to be happy over the next few months and beyond without things like this dragging me down.

In the end I decided to just stick to what I knew the best, and that was classroom teaching. I therefore decided to carry on with supply teaching until the New Year and hoped to try and find something a bit more permanent thereafter. Throughout this whole period I hoped to spend more time with our child by working part time.

On Friday, September 5th, Rav and I visited the City Hospital for her last baby scan at 32 weeks, so we got to see another glimpse of the new life that would be joining us very soon. Seeing the child actually yawn on the monitor made it even more real now. In a few weeks' time, we would both become parents and I would become a father myself. A few weeks before the due date Rav and I also attended an antenatal session together. I found the session quite helpful as it prepared both of us for the labour, birth and early parenthood stage. However, being at the session with Rav and seeing all the other partners to be left me feeling quite anxious. Although, on the outside it may have appeared that I was uninterested. Inside I was feeling worried about the future that lay ahead of me. I was worried about whether I could live up to being a father. What if I succumbed to the problems that my father faced? What if I wasn't able to bring my new child up the way my father did with me? What if I didn't bond with the new child? What if I could not bond with the new child?

When Rav and I first found out she was pregnant we had decided not to find out the sex of the baby. However, in my mind I seemed to have imagined us having a boy, so all the things that I envisioned for the future had a boy in mind. This was not to say I didn't want a girl, or that I felt girls were inferior to boys. In my mind I had somewhat been replicating what my father and I had. Maybe, I thought, with a boy I could relive my own memories that I had with my own father.

But, what if we did have a girl? Would I then feel guilty for the boy we never had? Would that then leave me disappointed and wishing we had a boy? I guess deciding on not finding out the sex of the baby left me with many confusing possibilities to ponder. But then again would it matter either way which sex it was? We had no idea what the sex of the baby would be but we did have two names in mind to cater for either possibility.

I had by now spent the last seven months of my life preparing for the birth of the baby as well as also trying to generate interest for the Brian Clough statue in Derby.

On Thursday, September 18th 2008, Steve Bloomer was inducted into the National Football Museum's Hall of Fame. This year's annual ceremony was held at the Millennium Mayfair Hotel in London.

On the morning of Thursday, October 9th I logged onto my PC and opened the *This is Derbyshire* website to catch up with the latest local news. After a few seconds, a familiar face caught my attention. To my surprise Steve Bloomer was in the news again. To my even greater surprise the headline read, 'Fans are watching Steve Bloomer in Pride Park reception'. What did that even mean? Steve Bloomer was inside Pride Park? I clicked on the link and read on.

Fans of Derby County legend Steve Bloomer will soon be watching him as work begins on his commemorative bust.

'My goodness', I mouthed in amazement. Absolute confirmation. Steve Richards had well and truly done it.

Visitors to Pride Park over the next two weeks will be able to see the bronze sculpture under construction.

'Rav!', I shouted. A few moments later Rav emerged to see me sitting on the sofa with my laptop resting on my knees. 'What's up?', she asked, worried.

'Steve Bloomer, Steve Bloomer's getting a bust!', I replied.

Fans are watching Steve Bloomer in Pride Park reception

Thursday, October 9th, 2008 – *The Derby Telegraph*

Work to begin on sculpture of one of Derby County's best ever players.

By Caroline Jones.

Fans of Derby County legend Steve Bloomer will soon be watching him – as work begins on his commemorative bust.

Visitors to Pride Park Stadium over the next two weeks will be able to see the bronze sculpture under construction.

Artist Andy Edwards, who created statues of Gordon Banks and Sir Stanley Matthews for Stoke City's Britannia Stadium, will start work tomorrow.

His progress can be monitored by fans who pass through the reception area of the Toyota West Stand.

Work may also continue during the Rams' home match against Plymouth Argyle on Saturday, October 18, to give match supporters a chance to see the progress.

Mr Edwards said: "It is a great honour to be asked by Derby County to work on this.

"I have had the privilege to be part of some pretty big projects in the past but this one is as prestigious as any.

"Steve Bloomer is a giant of football and this tribute will recognise his standing in the game."

Fans have been raising the £17,000 needed for the tribute since 2003 and they, with financial help from Derby County hit the target in August.

The statue is set to be unveiled in January to coincide with Steve Bloomer's 135th birthday and the 125th anniversary year of Derby County's formation.

Derby County president and chief executive Tom Glick said it was the perfect way to remember the player's legacy.

He said: "Steve Bloomer is a name that will forever be integral with Derby County and it's time to give his memory a fitting and lasting tribute.

"We are very proud to lead this project on behalf of supporters past, present and future to ensure that Steve's legacy to football is never forgotten.

"This is a project inspired by the fans, for the fans and an opportunity to become involved with recognising one of the greatest players in this club's history."

Steve Bloomer played for Derby between 1892 and 1914, scoring 332 goals. He also notched up 28 goals for England in 23 matches. He died in 1938.

Fans dedicated a song to him, Steve Bloomer's Watching, played at each game.

Earlier this year, his name was on the list of nine inductees to the National Football Museum's Hall of Fame.

Hodgkinson Builders will build the bust's plinth, which will include stone from the old Baseball Ground, and it will stand next to the home dugout.

The most recent donation towards the statue came from lifelong fan Ian Hodgkinson.

He agreed to spend £857 the total number of Bloomer's Rams goals and appearances on a painting of the legend.

The painting was produced by Mr Edwards using Toyota car spray paints and donated to the club to help raise funds for the project.

Mr Hodgkinson said: "The entire project is breathtaking.

"It's a very bold statement from the club about their commitment to Derby's heritage."

On Monday, October 13th, I decided to head down to Pride Park to try and get an early glimpse of the creation of the Steve Bloomer bust in progress. Having read about the story in the *Derby Evening Telegraph* on the previous Thursday I had excitedly waited for Monday to arrive. I desperately wanted to be somehow involved in this project and contribute as much as I could, but I was also very apprehensive as to whether my involvement would be appreciated or even accepted. There was only one way to find out. On this particular Monday I decided to take Rav with me for company, so that I could meet the sculptor Andrew Edwards face to face.

As we entered the reception doors I immediately noticed a clay miniature of the Steve Bloomer bust placed on the reception table. A tall man called Sid Marson, then stood up from behind the reception desk to ask if I needed any assistance. I told him that my wife and I had come in to see Andrew Edwards working on the Steve Bloomer bust. Sid smiled, looked over towards the sculptor and then sat back down.

I turned to Andrew Edwards and introduced myself and then Rav; he then introduced himself as Andy. He wiped the wet clay off his hand and shook my outstretched hand. It was at this point that I properly caught sight of the actual Steve Bloomer bust for the first time. The bust was in its early stages as a skeletal structure made of what seemed like chicken wire formed into the shape of the upper half of a man's body with his arms folded. The smaller maquette figure of the bust also made in clay showed what the finished piece would eventually look like. The arms folded pose was quite familiar to me as I was very aware of the original photo it had been based on. The skeletal structure made from wire, wood and scraps of newspaper had already had some clay added to it.

As Andy and I began to talk about the process of creation he also continued to add clay to the skeletal structure of the bust.

Rav had, by now, decided to sit down near the trophy cabinet as she had clearly seen how involved and excited I had become whilst chatting to Andy in deep conversation. I had told her before we arrived that we would not be staying for too long and straight after I had seen the bust in progress we would pop into Mothercare, in the Wyvern Centre to pick up a few extra last minute items.

As Andy continued to flesh out the torso of the bust I watched on and began to realise that Steve Bloomer was literally being brought back to life before me, piece by rolled up clay piece. At one point, Andy even allowed me to add to the bust myself. At first I was reluctant to do so, thinking even the addition of the smallest amount of clay would ruin the final piece. That is the last thing I ever wanted. But after a further moment's hesitation I yielded and then pulled off a minimal amount of clay from a piece that Andy had given to me. I then carefully applied and worked this into the bust's face.

I was so overjoyed to have met Andy, and to have also made a small contribution to the construction of the bust, which was now indeed taking shape before my eyes. I was also very touched by Andy's kindness towards me. He obviously saw in me, someone like him who only ever wanted to see the absolute best final product for the Steve Bloomer bust that he was creating. I began to beam with happiness as I looked over at Rav and smiled. I then called her over to ask if she could take some pictures of Andy, the bust and myself. It must have been the first time in a very long time that she had seen me smiling so unreservedly.

I couldn't wait to see the final version and knowing that Andy would be at Pride Park for the next few weeks perfecting the bust in clay. I would definitely be back over the next few days and weeks.

During my first visit to see Andy Edwards working on the Steve Bloomer bust I also managed to spend some time chatting to Sid Marson who was sat close by as Andy and I talked. I was not the only fan wanting to see the bust creation in progress that day so as more fans came in I would briefly stop chatting to Andy to allow them to also speak to him. It was during these moments that I was then able to have little chats with Sid.

As I chatted to Sid I found out that he had been working for Derby County Football Club for nearly 50 years. So that meant that virtually any football fan that had ever passed through the turnstiles at the old Baseball Ground and then Pride Park Stadium would no doubt have been quite familiar with Sid over all these years. Since 1961, he had worked for the club as a chief steward, ground safety officer and also a Pride Park Stadium tour guide; he had started the tours in 1998 with his help from his wife Barbara.

Sid had first started going to the Baseball Ground with his father as a child and then in 1961 when Sid was 30 he began working on the turnstiles. Over the next few years he was then promoted to turnstile supervisor and then made ground safety officer after the Bradford fire disaster that occurred on Saturday, May 11th 1985. He then became chief steward at the Baseball Ground and, when the move to Pride Park occurred he took charge of the corporate boxes.

Sid and Barbara would also to go to matches at the Baseball ground together and then because he was working there, Barbara would also take along their two sons. The two sons also later worked at the club and so did Sid's brother Keith.

On leaving reception that day I just knew that my story would have a great ending. Steve Bloomer had returned back into my life nearly 20 years after I first stumbled across his name. I also realised that I had found a kindred spirit in my new friend Andy, the clay man from the potteries. A Blurton-born sculptor who was clearly very proud of his roots back home.

Andy was born in Stoke-on-Trent in 1964 and graduated from Staffordshire University in 1986. After graduating he spent seven years working within the special effects industries, working in puppetry and model making at the studios of Madame Tussauds. He has also worked as a figurative sculptor, artist and precision model maker.

I bid goodbye to Sid and Andy and told them I would be back. I also left my contact details with Andy so that we could keep in touch on email and exchange further information and photos in relation to Steve Bloomer that I had been collecting over the last few months.

The next day on Tuesday, October 14th I returned to Pride Park alone although I did bring some books with me; Peter Seddon's Steve Bloomer biography and another one I had only recently purchased called *Derby County: Player of the Year* by Jim Fearn. I brought the second book along with me in the hope that Sid would sign his name in it.

When I asked Sid for his autograph that day, he initially thought I was taking the mick. But when he realised I was being serious he began to almost blush. In my opinion he was as much a part of Derby County Football Club as all the great players that had once played for our team over the years. He had seen and lived through so much and yet he remained loyal, just like another Derby County stalwart by the name of Gordon Guthrie who had been at the club even longer as a player, former physio and now kitman. Sid had given his life to our club and I felt it was important for him to know that fans like me appreciated just how much he had contributed. Players and managers all got recognised and Sid deserved the same in my book.

On this day I stayed at Pride Park much longer than I had done the previous day. This also gave me time to explain to Andy just how much Steve Bloomer meant to me and why I so desperately wanted to leave my mark on the Steve Bloomer bust. I also showed Andy Peter Seddon's biography and then explained to him my whole story about the loss of my father by suicide and Steve Bloomer's involvement in the story I was writing up. Andy listened on intently and began to understand why the Steve Bloomer bust mattered so much to me. He had also lost his father and could therefore understand my loss too.

We talked a great deal that day, I also informed Andy of the plans to erect a Brian Clough statue in Derby that I hoped the club would similarly get behind like they had done with the Steve Bloomer bust. I also revealed to Andy that it was my hope that Peter Taylor would stand shoulder to shoulder beside Brian Clough one day too.

During our conversations there was so much we were learning from one another. I would fill Andy with information and he would likewise fill me with knowledge about things I didn't even know about or knew very little about. In relation to Steve Bloomer, Andy had done his homework but I still knew just a little bit more. I knew more because I had read Peter Seddon's biography. I therefore decided to buy Andy a copy from Waterstones. I also made sure to pass on as many photos of Steve Bloomer as I could which I had found on the Internet for research purposes.

From the moment I met Andy I knew that I had to do all I could to assist him with anything he needed in relation to the construction of the bust. Andy also told me about all the other statues that he had been involved in. Two in particular that really interested me were Sir Stanley Matthews and Gordon Banks at the Britannia Stadium, Stoke City F.C.

The Sir Stanley Matthews statue was sculpted by Andy Edwards, Julian Jeffrey and Carl Payne, which included three nine-foot statues showing Sir Stanley Matthews at different stages of his football career. They spanned more than 30 years. The location of the statue was at the Britannia Stadium but actually pointed towards Stoke City F.C.'s old Victoria Ground where Sir Stanley used to play.

The Gordon Banks statue that was created by Andy was also housed at the Britannia Stadium and had been unveiled only a few months previously by Pelé.

When I left Pride Park that day I made a quick visit into town to purchase another Steve Bloomer biography for Andy. I then went home and made plans with Rav to drive to Stoke the next day. I just had to see Andy's work up close to get an idea of just how good Steve Bloomer's bust could be.

The next day on Wednesday, October 15th, Rav and I once again visited Pride Park to see Andy and the Steve Bloomer bust. After I gifted Andy a copy of the Steve Bloomer biography I told him that we wouldn't be hanging around for too long because Rav and I had made plans to drive up to Stoke to see his Sir Stanley Matthews and Gordon Banks statues at the Britannia Stadium. Andy looked really chuffed and full of smiles when I told him this.

As Rav and I were leaving Barbara and Sid popped into reception to also have a look at how the bust was progressing. Sid then introduced his wife to us all and I then took some pictures of Sid and Barbara standing next to the Bloomer bust for them. Rav and I then left for the Britannia Stadium.

At this moment in time Rav was only a week away from her due date and was heavily pregnant. But we both needed to get out of the house and have her walking about. So although visiting the Britannia Stadium might not have been her cup of tea, it did do the pair of us some good. On arrival at the stadium we both spent some time looking at the Sir Stanley Matthews statue and having our photos taken with it. We then both popped into the reception of the club to see the Gordon Banks statue and this time I alone stood next to Gordon holding the World Cup aloft with him. The quality of the workmanship into all the statues was quite amazing and they definitely looked like who they were supposed to be. From that moment on I knew Steve Bloomer would be in good hands with Andy Edwards.

There was another reason why I decided to go into Stoke with Rav. As the due date was fast approaching I also needed to keep myself busy. In my mind there was so much that could still go wrong and I wouldn't be 100% at ease until the baby was born and I knew that the child was in good health.

The visit to Stoke was a distraction to the anxieties that continued to build within me. But Steve Bloomer had helped me a lot to reduce them over the last few days when I first heard that a bust of him was in the process of being created. Steve Bloomer had kept me distracted.

That afternoon, when Rav and I returned home, I made sure to share the Stoke photos on Facebook with all my friends as well as send them to Andy via email. I also added Sid Marson as a friend on Facebook.

Over the next few days I continued to keep myself busy, by visiting Andy at Pride Park as well as doing some more reading. Andy and I also continued chatting to each other via email; sharing information and photos that would help with his research.

On Monday, October 20th I decided to pay a visit to my old Mackworth College. I'd recently found out that an ex Derby County player by the name of Steve Powell worked at the gym there. The reason I went to visit him was because I had also found out that his late father Tommy Powell who also played for Derby County F.C. had for many years kept an autograph of Steve Bloomer in his wallet. I had some time to kill, so I decided to pay Steve a visit and get a photograph taken with him too. It was great to meet him that day and talk about his own career as a two-time First Division winner with Derby County F.C. As well as talk to him about the Steve Bloomer autograph that his father Tommy once managed to obtain from the great man.

A few hours after I had got home Rav phoned the City Hospital because she began experiencing irregular contractions, and she was told to come in. After a couple of hours waiting in the hospital and Rav getting tested we were told that the baby was not quite ready to be delivered yet and that we should call the hospital the next afternoon.

On the evening of Tuesday, October 21st, Rav was ready to give birth at the Derby City Hospital. The previous night's premature visit to the hospital had meant we already had all our bags packed for the big occasion. I also brought my own rucksack, which contained my MP3 music player, mobile phone and a couple of Derby County F.C. books I decided to bring along with me so that I could read as we waited. I was also wearing my black Derby County F.C. hoodie and a limited edition metal pin badge in the shape of Brian Clough's famous green sweatshirt.

I had bought two of these tribute pin badges, which had 'Be Good' Brian Clough, written on them. They were originally sold to raise money for the Nottingham Brian Clough Statue fund.

During that evening I also listened to Derby County F.C. playing away at Blackpool on BBC Radio Derby. Derby County F.C. lost 3-2.

Rav had been initially placed in a room with six beds. But we seemed to be the only ones in there while Rav waited to be induced to encourage regular contractions. As we both waited I decided to make a start on finishing the book I had bought the other week. The one I got Sid Marson to sign, *Derby County: Player of the Year* by Jim Fearn. So, I spent the rest of the night and very early morning reading through the various player profiles who had won the player of the year award since Roy McFarland had first won it in the 1968–69 season. Reading Martin Taylor's profile from the 1993–94 season brought back some good memories. As I was reading from the book I continued to sip from my large bottle of energy drink as I kept an eye on Rav to see how she was doing. Throughout the night Rav told her midwife that she was experiencing contractions. For whatever reason though, they didn't believe she was having any contractions. Rav kept telling me she was intense pain, but what could I do? Fortunately she got through the night even though there was nobody checking up on her. Eventually, the next morning on Wednesday, October 22nd a new midwife came on shift, listened to what Rav was saying and waited with her until she experienced her next contraction. And it was only then that we were moved into a new room ready for the birth.

I had been sat with Rav awake, nearly all through the previous night and then into the next morning. The new baby was taking its time. Around midday Rav suggested to me that I should go home for a couple of hours to get myself something to eat because all I had eaten in the last few hours was a piece of toast that I pilfered from the breakfast Rav couldn't face eating. So, reluctantly I decided to go home. Rav was now in a more comfortable state having also been given some gas to ease her pain. She was now joined by another midwife and a trainee doctor. I decided to go home because I knew that she would now be regularly checked up on.

A couple of hours later I was returning to the hospital with a spring in my step, having eaten, rested and freshened up. Today was definitely going to be the arrival of the new baby, I just knew it.

As I approached Rav's room I was still smiling. Just as I was about to step in I saw an empty room with no hospital bed. I then looked down and saw Rav's slippers still on the floor. So I popped my head into the room and looked left then right. 'Where's Rav?', I thought to myself. My smile disappeared. Confusion overwhelmed me. 'Where's my wife', I ask myself. 'Quick, put these on', a voice from behind me instructed. 'Where's my wife?', I ask the nurse as I take the overalls from her. 'You can change in that room over there', she said. I emerged from the room with the overalls over my clothes. 'She's been taken into the emergency operation room', I am informed. 'She's having a baby', I think to myself. 'We had to rush her in as the baby's heartbeat dropped', she tells me. 'Dropped, what does that mean? The baby has no heartbeat?' I think to myself. I'm led towards the emergency operation room. As I walk towards the door I begin to question myself. 'Why? Are we going to lose our baby? Why me? What have I done to deserve this life? Not again. I can't take another loss. The baby? My wife?'. 'Help me', I have no idea who I am directing my question to. Am I asking my father? Am I asking a higher power? 'Help me. I can't take any more death'. There is no time to get upset. As bad as it gets I must go through that door and face whatever comes. I approach the door then raise my right fist towards my chin and then throw my elbow and forearm into it and let my body whole fall straight through. The rest of my life will be determined by what happens on the other side.

I see a hospital bed in front of me with Rav stretched out on it with her back to me. Doctors and nurses crowd around her ready to operate. Rav's body turns, her head follows and then her eyes finally roll over and look at me, 'Kally what's happening?' she calls out dazed and confused. 'It's ok, don't worry. Everything will be all right', I reply unknowingly.

Suddenly everything stops. Everyone stops. 'It's a false alarm', I hear to my relief. Rav doesn't need to be operated on. The leads that had been attached to her to monitor the baby's heartbeat had become detached. That's why the heartbeat had dropped and was not registering. Rav's hospital bed is wheeled back into the room she had been placed in earlier.

About nine hours later a child was born, followed by a little scream. It is 23:15 on Wednesday, October 22nd 2008. I quickly take a photo of the clock and a few more of the baby's first moments after birth. I look upon mesmerised. I'm too overcome by the birth of the child as I stare at its face. It takes me a good few seconds to inform Rav what the sex of the baby is. 'What is it?', Rav asks again. I look down beyond the umbilical cord. 'It's a girl', I tell Rav. Rav holds our new baby for the first time and the umbilical cord is cut.

The baby is taken off her and patted down with a towel and then weighed on the scales at 6lbs 1oz. Another clean towel is then wrapped around her. I take the Brian Clough pin badge off my hoodie and place it on the towel close to my little girl's face as I take a photo. I pick my child up for the very first time and bring her face close to mine. 'I can hear your heartbeat', I whisper into her ear as a tear rolls down my cheek.

Chapter 24: Lost & Found

Everything is wonderful.

Rav and I decide to name our child Layla. We always only ever had two names in mind. Rohan if it was a boy and Layla if it had been a girl. We'd both been very keen on the name Layla, myself even more so because of my love for the song Layla by the blues-rock band, Derek and the Dominos. I'd been listening to the song a lot in the days before her birth and especially the guitar playing of Eric Clapton. Prior to Layla's birth I was becoming very worried and anxious, hoping that everything would work out fine and trouble free. Although, it didn't quite go as planned when the time came. There was obviously a big scare, but in the end Layla's birth did indeed ease my worried mind.

Layla Anise Mohin Kaur Dhindsa became her full name. I always wanted part of my father's name to be part of her new name. That is why Mohin was added as a nod to my father Mohinder. The Anise was added as an afterthought when I realised that the initials LMKD almost spelled out lamb. It was therefore only right to add the A making the initials LAMKD, especially considering the name of the senior midwife, Mary who helped to deliver Layla. This was also a nod to the Derby Ram. Another great coincidence of the birth date was that Layla had also been born exactly a year to the day that Steve Bloomer and I had first appeared in the Derby Evening Telegraph together.

Not long after the birth I left Layla and Rav and decided to go outside and make a call to my mother and inform her of the birth of our newborn baby girl. It didn't take her long to pick up the phone and I was relieved to tell her that everything was fine. I returned to Rav and Layla and spent a couple more hours in their company before I decided to go home and come back the next morning when we had all rested.

When I got home I decided to upload some photos onto Facebook as well as share the news about the birth of Layla.

Rav and Layla spent the next two days together at the hospital. During this time, close family members also came to visit and offer their congratulations. On Friday, October 24th 2008, Rav and Layla were finally allowed to go home. Although, we didn't go to our own home immediately; instead, I decided to first visit my old home in Pear Tree.

When we arrived, I carried Layla through the front door in her car seat.

That night when we had all returned home I lay on the bed with Layla beside me, watching, smiling and unbelieving. I was a father to this child. Such a small child, yet she would grow and age, but all that seemed so far into the distant future. Rav brought me a sandwich on a plate and placed it on the bed next to us, before I could even take a bite out of it Layla had already put her foot in it.

Over the next few days I continued to visit Andy at Pride Park and checked up on the progress of the Steve Bloomer bust. During the course of this period I also got to know more about Andy, his work and also his love of football. He was a big Stoke City F.C. fan and shared numerous stories about his and his father's heroes. Andy had met many of them over the years through his work or heard stories about them from his father. Players such as Sir Stanley Matthews, Frank Soo, Gordon Banks, Denis Smith, Terry Conroy and many more. He also told me about the likes of Josiah Wedgwood and Slash from Guns N' Roses and their connection to the potteries.

Our conversations would continue away from Pride Park too as we regularly emailed each other to discuss ideas and thoughts that we had touched upon during our chats. Sometimes I would go home to do further research to help Andy out by finding photos on the Internet that would assist him with issues he was pondering. No stone was left unturned to help bring our mutual hero back to life. Every protruding vein on Bloomer's arms and the buttons and wrinkles on his shirt were carefully and thoughtfully sculpted into place. The final product had to look as real and lifelike as possible. There could be no cutting corners. At one point, Andy became a little unsure as to how to proceed on Bloomer's hairline. It was a difficult one to get our heads around. Although there were many photos of Steve Bloomer in the archives, there were none we could find of the back of his head.

I reflected on the problem when I got home having pondered on it with Andy earlier in the day. After spending a couple of hours searching on the Internet for more photos I realised that I couldn't find any more that could help us. I began looking for photos of other players that would have played in the same era, the Victorian era. But that didn't help either although it did make me think down the road of royalty.

Queen Victoria had passed away on Tuesday, January 22nd 1901 to be then immediately succeeded by King Edward VII. I began searching for images of King Edward VII and whilst I was doing that I caught sight of a coin with his side profile on it. And there was the answer. Steve Bloomer's hairline could be modeled on the hairlines of the Kings who reigned in the era that Steve Bloomer played in. The answer was in the coin. I immediately emailed Andy and shared some coin images of King Edward VII and King George V. Andy quickly replied and agreed that it was only right that Steve Bloomer's hairline should be modelled in the likeness of a king. After all, Steve Bloomer was indeed the first king of English football goal scorers.

On Thursday, November 6th about two weeks after Layla was born, I decided to take Rav and Layla down to Nottingham. It was the day of the Brian Clough statue unveiling and I didn't want to miss it for the world. Sib also wanted to see the unveiling so he joined us on the trip to Nottingham from Derby.

A statue to Brian Clough had already been unveiled in his hometown of Middlesbrough in the previous year. It was now Nottingham's turn to unveil their own. On this day the statue was unveiled by Brian Clough's widow Barbara in the company of several members of the Clough family as well as a few thousand more people in attendance including fundraisers, the media, ex players who were once managed by Brian Clough and of course his many fans.

One of the fundraisers was a hardcore Nottingham Forest fan by the name of Rich Fisher. In his very younger days Rich had also published the Forest Forever fanzine in the 1990s. I was already aware of Rich and his brother Al as both of them were frequent users of a Nottingham Forest Forum website called Lost That Loving Feeling. I first engaged with the pair of them on this forum making it quite clear from the beginning that I was a Derby County fan trying to promote a petition for a Brian Clough Statue in Derby. Fortunately for me, Rich and Al were real football fans who immediately recognised what I was trying to do and were very helpful in promoting the cause as well as collecting many more signatures for the campaign. We may have supported different teams, but Brian Clough united us all.

As Sib and I inched ourselves forward to get a better view of the unveiling, Rav stood further back from the huge crowds and remained with Layla in her push chair. It was only after the statue was unveiled and I saw the beautiful statue in all it's splendor that a feeling of awkward upset and discomfort then filled my stomach. I was gutted. Yes, it was great to see Les Johnson's Brian Clough statue unveiled and to see Brian Clough rightly decorated and recognised by the people of Nottingham but it was also a great shame to me that Peter Taylor was not standing by his side and also being honoured in the same way. In my opinion Clough and Taylor were a team and they both contributed equally to the success that Nottingham Forest F.C. enjoyed during the magical six-year period that their partnership spanned. More than that though, I knew full well that Peter Taylor was a Nottingham-born man. How was it possible that his people in Nottingham did not feel the same way? Was he now really a forgotten hero? He should have been standing alongside Brian Clough as I was trying to do by uniting the pair in Derby with our own statue campaign. As the crowds began to slowly disperse Sib and I made our way to the statue to have a closer look as well as take some photos.

By now I'd also seen Nigel Clough still hanging around, talking to the fans, so I thought I would try and get a photo taken with him too. I patiently waited until the opportunity arose and when it did I took off my jacket and handed it over to Sib. When I approached Nigel he was a bit taken aback to see that as I was wearing my Derby County F.C. jersey in the middle of Nottingham. I had a brief conversation with him and told him about our plans in Derby to erect a statue of his father as well as one hopefully for Peter Taylor too. I then handed him a flyer for the campaign. He told me that he had heard of the plans and that he wished us all well. Sib took a photo of the two of us together. As well as one more of me turning my back to the camera so that Sib could take a photo of the back of my jersey standing next to Nigel Clough looking on. On the back of my jersey I had printed CLOUGH on the top, a large number 1 in the middle and then below that, TAYLOR upside down. In my eyes Clough and Taylor were a partnership. The best ever and they deserved to be recognised as one.

I was so grateful to have met Nigel Clough that day and to be able to speak to him as well as share plans for our statue campaign in Derby. As I was also carrying a book with me on the off chance I might collect some autographs, I asked Nigel if he could sign his autograph on a particular profile page for me. When he said yes, I quickly passed him my copy of *The Legends of Derby County* by Ian Hall and a black sharpie pen. I asked if he would sign his name alongside his father's profile photo. Nigel duly obliged 'Best Wishes Nigel Clough'. On saying goodbye to him and shaking his hand I quickly put my jacket back on. However, a couple of knuckleheads in the crowd had seen me in my Derby County F.C. jersey and had taken great offence. In harsh tones they advised me to leave their city immediately. I wasn't deterred by their aggressive behaviour though. I just laughed them off. I couldn't stop laughing at the way they were pronouncing the word 'city'. I was a little happier now. I had met Nigel and the gut feeling I had earlier had somewhat subsided. But I knew exactly what I had to do when I got back home into Derby. I would talk to Ashley Wilkinson and convince him to change the petition and have Peter Taylor on board too. In my opinion our statue in Derby was going to be Clough AND TAYLOR or nothing at all.

On my next return to Pride Park to meet Andy I told him about the statue unveiling in Nottingham to Brian Clough and how it made me feel. It wasn't right that Peter Taylor should be forgotten like this. He contributed just as much. He had a family, he must have had children too. How would they be feeling that their father seemed to have been forgotten. It wasn't fair. As I was telling Andy this he stopped working on the Bloomer bust and then took a backward step in deep thought. I pointed out the window. 'We could have a statue of Clough and Taylor right over there', I told him. Andy smiled, 'Yes, we could. Clough and Taylor'. I looked on and watched Andy thinking and smiling to himself as he stroked wet clay into his chin.

The Steve Bloomer bust had been progressing so well that even Andy was now turning his attention to a possible Clough and Taylor statue that he could propose to the club and make himself. Andy Edwards was most definitely the right man for the job and the club now knew that too.

A few months after the Brian Clough Statue unveiling in Nottingham, Ashley Wilkinson received an email from a lady called Wendy Dickinson via the online petition. By now Ashley had already changed the petition title to 'Brian Clough & Peter Taylor Statue Outside Pride Park Stadium, Derby'. With the buzz about the film of 'The Damned United' also occurring around the same time. Peter Taylor had once again been brought into the public limelight as football fans from all clubs were once again reminded of the immense contribution Taylor had made in the Clough and Taylor partnership. It is no wonder then that when Wendy Dickinson heard that there was a campaign to recognise and honour her father with a statue of Clough and Taylor in Derby she, her brother Philip and their mother Lilian were fully behind our Derby campaign.

After a good few weeks of being almost camped out at Pride Park on Friday, November 14th 2008 Andy and the Steve Bloomer bust would be spending their last day in reception and leaving to make their way to the foundry so that the bust could be cast in bronze.

I knew the day would eventually come, but what a great journey it had all been in these last few weeks. Finding out that Derby County F.C. were going to build a bust, meeting Andy, working with him, discovering more statues, campaigning for new ones, the birth of Layla, seeing the Brian Clough unveiling in Nottingham and now seeing the finished Steve Bloomer bust in clay.

I would like to think that I had contributed something special to the Steve Bloomer bust. Andy certainly appreciated what I had done for him and Bloomer, as he gave me a signed wooden calliper as a gift, which he'd used to construct the bust in the early stages.

On the penultimate day at Pride Park I pondered whether I should ask Andy if I could add one more thing to the bust. I wanted to leave my mark to honour my great hero and the area Steve Bloomer, my father and myself all grew up in. Andy and I had struck up such a good friendship by now that I just came out with it. 'Andy, you know how much this guy meant to me. And how much I appreciate you allowing me to contribute to his creation. Well, would it be possible if I could add something to him? A subtle little something just under his left elbow to recognise where he came from?'. Andy looked at me and laughed, 'Of course Kal, bring it in tomorrow. It would be my pleasure'. I couldn't believe it. What a lovely thing for him to allow me to do.

Andy's approach to his art featured a journalistic quality because he used his sculpture to convey a story, idea or reflect a point in history. Research and historical accuracy were obviously a vital part of his creative process; his attention to detail and passion for the story behind the work was the driving force for all his sculptures. Therefore, I shouldn't have been surprised one bit when he allowed me to contribute my own story to his work.

That afternoon I went home and drew some sketches on the back of an old receipt. Whatever I designed needed to be simple, small and subtle. I pulled out some pliers from my toolbox and then opened a pack of solder wire that I had purchased from B&Q. The design on the receipt was the shape of a pear to symbolise the old Pear Tree neighbourhood that Steve Bloomer, my father and myself had all grown up in. After a couple of efforts I had created a pear logo from the soft solder wire. I had done this by cutting a long piece of wire off then gradually forming it into a flat coil circle, which had a section looped over at the top for the shoulders. The stem of the pear was then produced by feeding the end of the solder wire through the hole between the shoulders and back out again. The final piece was only an inch long and half an inch wide, but it was a perfect pear.

The next day I took it to Pride Park and as Andy finished off the last touches to the Steve Bloomer bust I showed him what I had made. Andy took it off me then congratulated me for my effort. He then pushed it into the clay under Bloomer's left elbow and forearm. I then took some final photos and video footage of the Steve Bloomer bust in clay and respectfully said goodbye to Andy.

It had been Andy's belief that for public art to be relevant it must inspire people; it must have something worth saying. Steve Bloomer definitely had something to say. Andy's devotion to his work was clear from the moment I first met him. I felt honoured just to be in his company.

Over the next couple of months, we regularly kept in touch via email and Andy kept me informed as to how far down the line he was in terms of casting the bust.

I next met Andy on Friday, January 16th 2009, which was one day before the actual unveiling of the Steve Bloomer bust. On this day Andy had invited me down to Pride Park to see the bust being installed inside the stadium. I wasn't going to go down alone so I decided to take Rav and Layla with me. That day we met Sid Marson in the reception and he led Rav, Layla and myself onto the pitch. When we arrived pitch side I noticed a few other people that were also there to see the bust. They included John Vicars the club's Chief Operating Officer, Ian Hodgkinson from Hodgkinson Builders Ltd and Ian Hayes.

Ian Hodgkinson was a local businessman and bricklayer who had contributed funds towards the bust campaign. His company had also used their apprentice bricklayers to build the base for the Steve Bloomer bust that was created near the home dugout. The actual bricks that were used were the original bricks from the old Baseball Ground.

Ian Hayes was one of the main men behind the Steve Bloomer Project who led the campaign to honour Steve Bloomer.

I saw Andy inspecting the Bloomer bust then approached him and shook his hand. We then began talking about the finished piece. The finished Steve Bloomer bust looked amazing. The hairline, the eyes, the buttons, the wrinkles in the shirt, the lot. I looked down at where the pear that I had created had been placed – it was still there. Subtle and small, and not too obvious, but if you observed carefully you would see it. It was great to see the pear logo attached to Bloomer. Andy, Ian Hayes and myself then had some photos taken of us standing next to the bust. Rav also took some of me and Layla. I had brought along Peter Seddon's biography and placed that on Layla's car seat as she slept. I then took a photo of her and the bust together.

Seeing Steve Bloomer attached to the bricks of the old baseball wall was a great sight to see. Another beautiful thing to observe was a replica of the Steve Bloomer tablet that used to be installed outside the director's entrance at the old Baseball Ground. A new cleaner version was now placed under the Steve Bloomer bust and also attached to the wall. The actual unveiling would be tomorrow, but the opportunity to see the bust installed meant that I could meet Andy and all the others who had contributed towards it too.

As we stepped back to see the bust from afar I noticed Sid Marson leading a group of school children towards the bust. He stopped. 'You all right, Kal?', he called out to me. 'These kids are from Pear Tree Juniors, I'm giving them a tour of the stadium'. My jaw dropped, what an unbelievable coincidence. Sid then began pointing out the pear logo to the children and then explaining to them how Steve Bloomer had also attended his first school in the Pear Tree area of Derby.

The day could not have gone any better. Nearly three years after the death of my father I had also become a father and had contributed towards erecting a bust for my great hero. I was also able to leave a small mark on the bust in recognition of the neighbourhood that I'd grown up in and would forever hold close to my heart no matter how far away I travelled from it.

On Saturday, January 17th the Steve Bloomer bust was unveiled at Pride Park. I had originally planned not to go down as I'd already seen my own unveiling of it with Layla and Rav the previous day. However, that morning I got a call from Sharon at the Great Northern Inn. She told me that Alan Quantrill and his family were down for the unveiling and were in the pub. They wanted to see me. Within no time at all I had driven down in my car to meet them all.

In the pub I got to meet Alan Quantrill, his wife and their son Richard. As I chatted to Alan Quantrill he spoke with great pride about his own footballing father Alfred Quantrill, who was born in Rawalpindi, Punjab – a Punjabi like myself I joked. As well as speaking about his legendary grandfather Steve Bloomer.

Alf Quantrill was the husband of Steve Bloomer's daughter, Hetty Winifred Bloomer.

Mr Quantrill was also very proud of the fact that both his father and grandfather represented the England National Football Team as well as Derby County Football Club.

I was told Steve Richards was also down for the day with his family to see the unveiling but he had already made his way to Pride Park. Richard Quantrill then surprised me by showing off the trophy that Steve Bloomer had been awarded by the National Football Museum Hall of Fame. It was a great honour for me to hold such an award.

Whilst in the company of the Quantrills I was also able to show Alan some moving pictures of Steve Bloomer that I'd found on YouTube. I also realised that this would probably be my only chance to meet Steve Richards too, so I decided to make my way down to Pride Park for the match; I knew that the *Rams Trust* would be able to provide me with a spare ticket for the game. Derby County F.C. were playing against Queens Park Rangers F.C. As I still had some time before the kick off I decided to park my car in Pear Tree then walk all the way to Pride Park for the match. It was a pleasant walk considering how far it was, but I had a lot on my mind. A lot of good things. I even took a detour so that I could pass the Brian Clough mural on Elton Road.

When I arrived at Pride Park I collected my ticket and made my way into the stadium. From my seat in the East Stand I could see people congregating near the dugouts just before kick off for the unveiling of the bust. I also managed to see Andy Edwards and all the other people who had contributed to the bust campaign. It was easy to see because I had also brought along my binoculars. When the moment of the unveiling came I saw Alan Quantrill and Steve Richards pull away the fabric over their grandfather's bust and reveal the new bust to the whole stadium.

Steve Bloomer's grandsons had done it. I was very pleased for them. At the end of the match, I made my way back to Pear Tree. As I did so I walked past the reception area at the front of the stadium. On doing so I caught a glimpse of Alan Quantrill. Who then beckoned me into the reception area. He then kindly invited me in to meet other members of the extended Bloomer family. It was here I was able to finally meet Steve Richards and tell him how much of a great hero Steve Bloomer had always been to me in my life; how we were both raised in the same area and how I was planning to write a story about him in which he would essentially be at the heart of.

It was a great honour for me to meet the whole family. Steve Richards even signed my copy of Peter Seddon's biography of Steve Bloomer, which I had been carrying in my bag along with my binoculars.

Steve Richards
Grandson of Steve Bloomer
(with gratitude)

I also managed to get a picture taken with Alan Quantrill and Steve Richards and saw for myself the love and respect both of them had for their beloved grandfather and his memory. Most of all I saw the great pride within them both as they finally saw their grandfather recognised for the hero he was and forever will be. Both grandsons had fought for years to make sure that Steve Bloomer's efforts and contribution to the game of football would be forever appreciated and never forgotten. It was thus quite fitting and touching that both of them finally got to see their grandfather receive the recognition he truly deserved by the people of Cradley, Derby, Derby County Football Club and the National Football Hall of Fame, within their own lifetimes.

It had been a great day for all of Steve Bloomer's family and all the fans that were at Pride Park to see the bust unveiled. After the unveiling of the bust Steve Richards said the following about his grandfather, 'Derby was his life and he would have been very honoured'.

I walked towards Pear Tree exhilarated. The return of Steve Bloomer that day had fixed many a little boy's broken heart. Not only his grandsons but maybe a small part of my own too. We had remembered him. As I walked, I reflected on all that I had achieved since my father's death.

Looking back, I would like to think that I had contributed in making people happy by remembering their loved ones from the past. That meant a lot to me and it felt good, yet, I knew that I still had much more to give. I was on top of the world. My attention from now on would be firmly on the Clough and Taylor campaign and then after that who knows. One thing was for sure; Layla and Rav would be by my side all the way.

Writing about my struggles had opened up another world for me. I was quite clearly on the right path now. Meeting Andy and being introduced to the world of sculpture gave me a further sense of purpose to keep me on that road to recovery. I had become a survivor of bereavement by suicide and although my story was far from over I knew I had to continue writing and share it with others as well as continue to help Andy make more statues to our heroes. Sculpture, like my writing, enabled me to bring things to life again, things from the past that may no longer have been with us. Andy had built a bust to my great hero. It was not a bust of my father, but it was as good as, for what that bust represented to me.

The story of Steve Bloomer and the journey to create a bust for him was the story of my father as well.

In my book, storytelling was very similar to sculpture. Andy had showed me that to sculpt something you had to ultimately discover a story first then slowly work backwards peeling layer by layer off until you unearth the seed of the artistic piece. The thing that gave it life and the true essence of sculpture. It is only then that you can truly make a start on the finished piece. It was just like writing but in reverse. In terms of my own writing and my own story I had begun with a seed. My title, *My Father & The Lost Legend of Pear Tree*. From this seed I had to add layers and layers until I finally discovered my own story. I still had a long way to go but I was on the right path, I just knew it. The foundations were all set; I was proud of who I was, where I came from and most importantly I wanted to desperately recognise the people who helped me get there.

Prior to meeting Andy I had very little faith that I could ever be involved in such a statue project. I would have felt that it was almost impossible for me to even try, never mind accomplish, but then I realised that so many things are possible just as long as you don't know they're impossible.

Andy Edwards and Steve Bloomer had showed me that all it took was a thought. The heart to want to make a difference. The guts to speak out and try and make that difference. And then finally the action to make that difference occur.

My father's suicide had brought my defenses crashing down. It took a long while until I was able to build them back up again. For a long time after his death, I used to get nervous when I saw an open door. I'm not afraid any more. The doors are now invitations into another world of possibilities.

Are we dreaming?

'Wake up Kal, he's here', the voice of football whispered into my ear.

'Who's here?, I asked.

'And what is John Motson doing in my bed', I thought to myself.

I was now sat up in my bed, fully clothed. I felt something close to my heart. I reached for it and then pulled it out of my breast pocket. It was a coin. It was Gian Singh's coin. The same coin he had given to me in Sahabpur. I put it back in my pocket and then looked around in the darkness.

The front door blew wide open as a gust of wind rushed into the house, followed by the sound of thousands of cheering fans. I hadn't heard those cheers in years, especially in Pear Tree. They seemed to be coming from the direction of the old Baseball Ground.

'Go home Kal', said the voice of football.

'But I am home', I replied.

In the very next second, I found myself strangely floating out of my bed and then down the stairs and out through the open front door into the night. My feet did not even touch the ground as I was slowly carried away from my house on the hill, towards a light through the darkness.

In the near distance I saw the backs of hundreds of marching Sherwood Foresters who had streamed out from the old Normanton Barracks. As I followed them towards the light the sound of the cheers became louder and louder the closer I was carried to the source. A shining bright light now lit up a path to the old ballpark followed by the sound of marching feet.

'Come on Kal, he's waiting, follow me', beckoned a black silhouette of a man.

A presence continued to carry me forward closely following the shadow ahead. We passed the nursery, the old Pear Tree schools, the Wallis clothing factory and then down towards the field. In no time at all we had arrived at Shaftesbury Crescent.

As we approached the Baseball Ground entrance the intense bright light of the Sunday morning sunrise began to consume the black silhouette of a man ahead of me.

I stopped at the entrance, where I had first seen Bloomer's tablet all those years ago, but it was not there and as soon as I realised this, the cheers evaporated into the night. A cuc-coo, coo pierced the silence.

Suddenly a shower-room door appeared from out of the old brickwork.

'Tokens please', a voice from the other side called out.

'But I don't have one', I replied as my feet softly touched down on the earth below.

'You sure kid? Come on now. Hand it over'.

I looked down at my hand and in my palm I was holding Gian Singh's coin again. I inspected it carefully. A Pear Tree on one side and a sideward profile of a face on the other. The word Ruhleben written above his head with the roman numerals 28 and 23 on either side. 1874 and Dum Spiro

Spero written below. The man on the coin then turned his head towards me and winked. There was no doubt about it. The watcher had been silently observing me all along.

The coin in my hand began to glow with a golden hue and then looking up I noticed that a slot had appeared in the shower room door. It was obviously a sign. So, I inserted the coin into the hole. The shower room door vanished and from behind it appeared a man with a lovely flapping moustache.

'Follow me kid, we've been expecting you. My name's Hudson. All the birds call me Chaz. You can call me Charles'.

I was led onto the Baseball Ground pitch, but it was not the field I expected. Yes, it was covered in luscious green grass, but it was not a football field, rectangular in shape, it was instead, a baseball diamond.

'Mr Kinsella has done a great job laying it out for us all to play ball on', said Charles.

'Wondrous Perfection', I replied, what a pretty park.

I began walking towards the pitcher's mound.

'He's been waiting for you', said a voice from behind me.

I looked back to see where it had come from. There was no one in sight but my shadow beneath me.

'Go on Kal'. I looked back down at my feet again and then noticed that my shadow had disappeared, even though the light still shone bright.

I looked up and a white silhouette of a man appeared in front of me. A face then emerged out of it. I recognised him immediately. It was Ben Warren. He had stepped out of the darkness and into the light. He looked happy, he smiled.

'He's been wanting to meet you for years … we all have', said Ben.

'Who Ben? Who?', I replied.

Ben stepped aside and in the distance, leaning against a brick wall, with his back to me. I saw him. 'It can't be …?', I whispered to myself. The man against the brick wall began to slowly turn his body and face towards me. I stood in awe, fixed to the spot. On seeing me he winked and nodded in acknowledgement. 'DERBY', blazoned across the chest of his pin stripe black and white baseball jersey.

'My Goodness. It was him', I heard myself say in disbelief.

Steve Bloomer had returned home just like the indomitable King of Rome.

I took a deep breath and grabbed the lapels of my jacket as I walked towards him. My saviour, the destroying angel now stood a few feet away, staring right back at me.

'I never forgot you Steve', I said to him.

He smiled and then grasped my hand with a firm handshake.

I smiled in relief, 'Thanks for always being there Steve'.

'No Kal. Thank you. You never gave up', replied Bloomer.

My eyes welled with tears, so I momentarily looked away but as I did so I noticed a sign above the coach's box. 'The Derby County Baseball Club'.

I looked back at Bloomer, intrigued. He then pointed towards the stadium tannoy.

'STEPHEN BLOOMER', called out the voice of football.

'BRIAN HOWARD CLOUGH'
'PETER THOMAS TAYLOR'
'DAVID CRAIG MACKAY'
'HUGH KILPATRICK GALLACHER'
'JOHN DAVID STAMPS'
'JOHN KIRBY'
'ALICE ANN WHEELDON'
'STEPHEN HENRY WETTON'

Mr Wetton ?!?! I said in astonishment. 'How's he made your team?'

Bloomer looked at me, surprised.

'Did he not tell you? He played for Derby County F.C. He was a Derby Boy', said Bloomer.

'Well he did, but we all thought he was pulling our leg', I replied.

'Good old Wetton. He loves telling stories. Never stops talking that one. Harry Storer recommended him to us, said he was a good catch. Young Steve has a good heart and always keeps our spirits high', said Bloomer.

I could not believe what I was hearing, I listened on in bewilderment, unsure whether Bloomer was being serious or not. 'He also wrote *Growing Pains* for the BBC you know?' At this point I burst out into a fit of laughter as I noticed Bloomer grinning at me.

Only when the last of my chuckles subsided did I then say to him in all seriousness, 'But Mr Wetton's not dead. What's he doing here?'.

'Everyone is welcome. No one is dead here, Kal. No one truly dies when their name is still spoken. Nobody dies in dreamland. Everybody lives'.

I began to choke up. 'Hey Steve, is this Heaven?', I asked.

Bloomer looked straight through me with his piercing grey eyes. The hairs on the back of my neck now stood to attention as a spark of electricity charged through my spine and out through my crown. I felt a hand on my shoulder from behind me, its fingers brushed my face.

'No son, it's Pear Tree. Thanks for looking after my boy, Steve', said my father.

'Kal Singh Dhindsa is our friend, Mohinder', Bloomer replied.

My father looked down at me, smiled and then bit his bottom lip.

'It's good to see you again Kally', he said as he hugged me. 'I missed you so much, Dad. I'm sorry I couldn't be there for you when you needed me', I said as I wept into his chest.

'It's ok, son. Don't worry. It's ok. I'm here. I never left you. Everything will be ok from now on', he said.

My father then pulled out a baseball from his parka pocket and placed it in my hand. 'I think you owe Steve this pitch'.

I was overcome with emotion and filled with pride. Steve Bloomer had brought my father home to me. 'Hey Steve! heads-up', I called out as I turned quickly on my heel and threw the baseball as hard as I could in his direction.

Steve Bloomer smashed it out of the ballpark.

He always did.

*

A saucepan boiled over in the distance.

'Mum must have the tea on, Dad?'.

'Let's go home son, we'll pick some milk up on the way back.

She'll be waiting for us'.

Epilogue

MY FATHER

My father didn't smile much, but when he did we knew he was happy. There was no better demonstration of this than when he would try to suppress a smile by biting back on his bottom lip when something tickled his funny bone. The biting of the lip was also a sign of his embarrassment too because during my very younger years I too was aware of the prominent gap between his two front upper teeth that he always tried to hide. He would later get this diastema closed but the habit of biting his lip would always remain.

My father was also an intelligent man with a great memory. A databox of sorts and everybody who knew him was aware of his amazing ability to remember birthdays and dates of special significance. You could ask him anything and he would be able to give you the time, date and place of when these events occurred, but this could also have been a side effect of his first brush with death in February 1993. Could the trauma of a brain injury have affected his mind in such a manner that it also improved his ability to remember things so vividly? Or maybe he always had a good memory? Whatever the explanation he made the most of what he had considering his limited vocabulary.

Although he was able to speak English reasonably well he also had a habit of making some strange faux pas such as getting his him and her pronouns mixed up during conversations. Growing up it was a great source of amusement in our family, when he would refer to both my mother and sister as him.

My father's limited education and his lack of confidence in his ability to speak English fluently held him back on many an occasion. There is no doubt that this played heavily on his mind all his life because he just didn't have the words to express himself as he hoped. It is no wonder that he would become snappy and frustrated when he wasn't able to communicate his thoughts properly whether that be in English or Punjabi.

I would on occasions also lose my temper with my father, but I always thought highly of him. On a few occasions in my life I may not have agreed with some of his decisions and what he did, but I always tried to defend him and not allow people speak badly of him. He shared some of my proudest moments with me, which in effect I hope were his too as I was his son. I only wish we could have shared more with each other. If only he knew how much I cared for him and how much it hurt me to see him struggling at times. He was my father and I loved him.

My father was very stubborn at times but that was his way, I guess much of that stubbornness has also rubbed off on me, but my hypocrisy goes only so far. My mother was quite different. Growing up, I despised the way she would effortlessly embarrass me and make me feel awkward and uncomfortable in front of others, but I guess in the long run this helped me because I'm now much more aware of how words and actions can be used to humiliate others. This is something I try my best to avoid doing, but also challenge when I see it happening to others. In life we can learn a lot from those around us, sometimes via positive experiences and sometimes unfortunately by negative experiences. I've learnt a lot from both my parents during these experiences. I've also learnt a lot from bad relationships with old friends, but in the end if you have learned something that becomes a positive through reverse learning, then you can't be too disheartened that you experienced the bad feelings in the first place.

Towards the end of my father's life I began noticing his dislike for technology more and more. It seemed the world around him was moving too fast for him and he just couldn't keep up. It was almost as if he just wanted to step off this world. He liked things the way they were done in the old days. Maybe he just wanted to be back in the old days again, with his brothers looking after him? He was quite obviously regressing and his memory was not as good as it used to be. I put that down to him not being interested any more, but what if it was something more? What if he was having serious issues with his memory? His greatest gift. Whatever it was, he was just not the same man any more he was definitely experiencing some form of mental tiredness.

I had forgiven my father for what he had done as his life was passing away before me in the hospital. He obviously did what he did because he couldn't bear life any longer. For whatever reason he felt his time was up and he had to go because living was causing him too much pain. I had to accept that even though I may not have fully understood what his reasons for doing what he did were at the time. But I had to let him know whilst he was alive that I had forgiven him for both our sakes. The last thing I wanted him to hear was me telling him how selfish I thought he had been.

I couldn't let my memory of him be allowed to disappear. All those photos and videos I still had of him I needed to keep safe just like the memories of him I still retained in my mind. He was my father and I owed it to him and my family to keep him alive within us all. Never to be forgotten. This was exactly the thought that continued to drive me forward, to remember him after his death. This thought also precipitated out of my dreams. The nightmare situation in which one day I should wake up and totally forget who he ever was. A life extinguished by suicide and then the possible corruption of my own mind via a mental illness.

I was already well aware of Alzheimer's and Parkinson's, having researched both of the diseases and the complications of dementia during my University years. In my mind I felt that Alzheimer's in particular was the harshest kind of illness that anybody could experience. To gradually forget all that you are and once were and the impact it has on your loved one as they also experience it with you.

I had to write it all down on paper, but now there was also another variable in the equation. Layla would one day have to be told of what happened to my father and what led to his death. I knew that day would come, but what would I say to explain it? I didn't want to lie to her. I didn't want to tell her an untruth. I've always tried to be honest with myself and I owed that to her too. But how do you explain something like that to a child? I just couldn't get my mind around it. I still had not come to terms with why my father died? I still had not found the answer to the question that tormented me still, 'Did he not love us?'.

THERAPY

The birth of Layla had made me question my own ability at being a good father. Could I be a good father to her like my own father was to me? Would Layla and I have the same relationship that I did with my father? For so long before her birth I had pictured in my mind that our child would be a boy. I had been trying to imagine my own relationship with my father being exactly the same with her after she was born.

I now found myself in a very confused place and riddled with anxieties about my family's future. I also felt insignificant and undeserving of all the things I had involved myself in. I felt as if people were looking down on me and sneering. 'That kid from Pear Tree should know his place. He has no business in trying to help others make statues and busts of great footballers from the past. It has nothing to do with him and he should keep his nose out'.

Thankfully I was able to continue to talk to Chris Roome about my anxieties and he helped me a great deal to overcome my periods of doubt. At one point I even took Rav and Layla in with me. I was trying so hard to not let myself down, to let my father down and most of all to not let Rav and Layla down. I needed guidance. I needed my father beside me. Thankfully with Chris's help I managed to work my way out of this darkness that I had once again fallen into. How did I do it? I just got back on the road to happiness that I had been rambling towards for the last couple of years. Fortunately, many of these roads led back to Pear Tree.

Chris was from Normanton like myself and another thing that we had in common was that I had taught one his nephews too. Therefore, it made it so much easier for me to talk and share with him what I was doing in my life and the various projects I was involved in. He always seemed genuinely interested. A perfect stranger who became a good friend to me and my family. I hadn't been speaking openly to anyone about my struggles up to this point. I had even held some of my problems back from Rav, as I didn't want to worry her. Unfortunately, I had by now realised that no matter how close you think you are to some of your family and friends, sometimes they just don't want to chat to you. Therefore, it was good to chat to Chris without having to try and put on a 'strong face'. It was ok to let your defences down to release your thoughts and feelings, and this made it easier for him to get through to me. As well as telling me that what I was going through was perfectly natural after such a bereavement and that I should be very proud of all that I have achieved since my father's death. It was great that he listened to what I had to say without ever judging me. This allowed me to reconnect with my fundamental beliefs in life, an understanding that you reap what you sow but before that you must first cast away your doubts.

'Our doubts are traitors, and make us lose the good we oft might win, by fearing to attempt'

Measure for Measure – (Act I, Scene IV)

William Shakespeare

I had to retain the faith that I had in myself and also the hope that I believed that I could one day get through all this and come out clean on the other side. At this moment in time I was in effect trapped in my own little Ruhleben, just like Steve Bloomer had been during World War I.

Steve Bloomer's incarceration in Ruhleben and his feelings of separation from Pear Tree mirrored my own. Those feelings would have become even more torturous for him when he found out about the death of his daughter Violet, back home in Portland Street. But the desire to return home to Pear Tree as well as continue to involve himself in football again at the camp, is what sustained him through his dark period.

'Dum Spiro Spero'

'While I breathe, I hope'

Motto on the Ruhleben coat of arms

My father was a good man. I refused to let him be forgotten so that's why I continued to write and speak about him when the opportunity to talk about suicide would arise. Whatever I did to remember him had to be a benefit to society. I would not let him die again. I could not let him die again. Suicide had already silenced him. It could have also silenced me too if I chose not to speak out about it. Suicide stops people talking. It was not going to stop me too, so I chose to write about it.

For this reason, I began to only engage in things that made me happy and stopped caring about what others thought of me. Everything I did from then on, I did for my father, which in the process continued to keep my spirits up. This was also one of the main reasons I kept returning to Pear Tree.

MINDY & MORK

On Tuesday, November 11th 2014 I returned home from work at Littleover Community School.

I had been working at the school on and off now since 2008 mainly covering maternity and paternity periods for members of staff in the science department. In between these stints I'd also worked as a Wireless Web Customer Consultant with the Carphone Warehouse and a Dyson Demonstrator at Currys. I was now back at the school working as a part time teacher of KS3 science as well as a science technician.

On this afternoon I sat down in the living room and then opened up my laptop to catch up with the latest news and goings on in the world. As I was doing this a photo of Robin Williams caught my attention.

Robin Williams had always been a great hero of mine ever since I first began watching him in the Mork & Mindy TV series. My mother and father also seemed to enjoy the show. I doubt they ever really got all the jokes but I'm sure they would have mainly laughed whenever they heard the name Mindy mentioned, as that was also one of my father's nicknames.

I had grown up watching Robin Williams and all the films that he had starred in. He was a magnificent actor and standup comedian who could make you cry and laugh in equal measure. Sometimes even cry in laughter, as his brilliant comedic talent would have you in absolute stitches. His starring roles in films such as Popeye, Good Morning, Vietnam, Dead Poets Society, Awakenings, Bicentennial Man, Insomnia and many more had really left their mark on me over the years.

I remember the day I found out that he had passed away. It was the early hours of Tuesday, August 12th 2014. I was sitting alone in the living room with my laptop open and noticed that his name was trending on Twitter. My heart sank a little, as every UK Twitter Trend was Robin Williams related. It didn't look good. I could sense that something of significance had occurred. I immediately Googled his name and my heart sank even further as I then read the news headlines. Robin Williams had died by suicide just like my father. The man who had brought so much laughter into this world was now no more.

He had passed away a few hours previously and the news of his death had travelled all over the world very quickly once it was confirmed. I sat in silence and reminisced. At first, I could only think about his suicide and kept thinking to myself, 'Why would he have done that?' But as in the case of my father I also knew that I might never find the answer. A few seconds later, I began smiling and chuckling to myself as I remembered all the times that he'd made me laugh during my younger years. He had died, but all I wanted to do now was remember how he'd lived and all the happiness he had brought into this world. It was the only way I could stop myself from becoming too upset about his passing and also thinking of my own father.

I clicked on the news story about his death. The headline read *Robin Williams' suicide 'was caused by hallucinations from a devastating form of dementia' he was battling alongside Parkinson's.* I paused and then the penny suddenly dropped from above. I was gobsmacked. Here in front of me was a possible reason as to why Robin Williams might have taken his life and thus died by suicide.

- Court documents revealed that Williams suffered from dementia with Lewy bodies.

- Sources say disease was the 'key factor' that drove him to take his own life.
- The legendary comic was found hanging from a belt at his home last August.
- Hallucinations are common among those affected by Lewy bodies dementia.

At this point tears started to well up as the weight of the world suddenly lifted from my shoulders. I had been carrying it for so long thinking that I would never be set free from the torment regarding my father's passing. But as soon as I read that headline my life took a turn for the better. As I wiped away the tears from my cheeks I continued to read the rest of the article. After Robin Williams' death in August 2014 it had originally been reported that he was suffering from severe depression, but as soon as this news about his dementia was revealed I immediately realised and accepted that he had died due to an illness. It was this mental illness that eventually led to his death.

My father had taken his own life and died by suicide on Wednesday, March 1st 2006, yet it was only now nearly eight and a half years later that I was finally able to accept that his death was also due to a mental illness just like Robin Williams.

It now became obvious to me that my father was not in full control of his thoughts; the illness as well as the side effects of his medicine had obviously combined together to permanently damage his ability to think straight and rationally.

For so long I was tormented by the question. 'Did he not love us? Why did he do it? Was it something I said? We said?' Robin Williams' death finally made me accept what I wanted to find out for so long. Not just an answer that I could accept without doubt but a possible reason as to why he did it. My father had died because of an illness; a mental illness that he could not overcome because his mind had been absolutely corrupted.

Lewy Body Dementia is a common form of dementia that can go undiagnosed in many patients experiencing dementia-like symptoms. The disease is caused by abnormal microscopic deposits that damage brain cells over time having been initially triggered by a previous traumatic head injury. This leads to a decline in thinking, reasoning and independent function.

The disease took its name from Frederick H. Lewy – the neurologist who discovered the brain abnormalities during the early 1900s. It shares symptoms with Parkinson's disease – sufferers can experience motor control problems, such as hunched posture, rigid muscles and a shuffling walk. Those affected can suffer visual hallucinations, which generally take the form of phantom objects, people or animals. It is also linked to Alzheimer's disease as it is more common over the age of 65 and those affected often suffer from confusion and memory loss.

I called out for Rav who was in the kitchen and showed her the article on my laptop. I then began reading the headline to her. *Robin Williams' suicide 'was caused by hallucinations from a devastating form of dementia' he was battling alongside Parkinson's.* 'Dad might have had this. I must tell Chris', I told Rav. She could see I was in an excited emotional state so didn't question me, but agreed that I should talk to Chris.

I immediately texted Chris from my mobile and explained what I had just read in the newspaper article. Chris replied back very quickly. He was aware of my father's background, as he had also been my father's mental health therapist. I had all but accepted my answer, but I wanted one further bit of medical support. Chris told me that it was impossible to know if my father had Lewy Body Dementia like Robin Williams as a detailed post mortem would not have been carried out on my father after his death, but it was quite possible that he could have had it or something similar. That is all I needed to know. The answer that I was seeking was not whether my father had Lewy Body Dementia for sure, but whether a dementia like illness was what led him to take his own life. My torment was over. Chris's answer was enough.

The symptoms that Robin Williams had been experiencing seemed to very much mirror that of my father's – the hallucinations in particular. The phantom aches and pains. As well as his confused state and issues with his memory.

Why did it take me so long to accept my father's death was the cause of a mental illness that had corrupted his mind? I knew he had depression, right? Yes, I knew he had depression but to me that was just not enough to fully accept, as the doubts always remained. What if he had taken his own life whilst his mind was still sane? The Daily Mail article had finally given me the information I needed to put my mind at rest and accept my father's suicide. It also supported the information on my father's death certificate; Cause of Death: Hanging High Suspension. Verdict: Suicide whilst the balance of his mind was disturbed.

I will forever be grateful to Robin Williams for allowing me to finally come to terms with my father's suicide. Gratefully, Mork had come back into my life to set the son of Mindy free.

Some people say that people who take their own lives by suicide are selfish. My father was never a selfish man. He always put others first. He was not selfish, what he did in terms of how he went about it could be considered to be a selfish act, especially in terms of all the heartbreak he left behind, but immediately after his passing I quickly realised that if I went around saying that my father was a selfish person because of his suicide then my relationship with him would have been totally finished in relation to whatever good I ever thought about him. If I had believed that at the time, I would never have forgiven myself for thinking such a thing. I wanted to remember him after his passing for all the good that he did in this world and not for how he left this world. You can only do that if you immediately accept that good people who die by suicide are not selfish.

It is quite clear to me now that when my father took his own life he would have done so having gone through his own brave and private battle with depression over a long period of time. In the end it just became too much for him, the last part of him that still wanted to hold on to his life had finally been completely corrupted and thus pushed him over the edge.

It is too easy to say that suicide is only for the weak and selfish. It just does not work like that. It is just not as black and white as that. There is only darkness for those who die by suicide.

MY FATHER & THE LOST LEGEND OF PEAR TREE

Steve Bloomer was a father to his children just like Mohinder Singh Dhindsa was to my siblings and me. In their own way they both made a meaningful contribution to the community they lived and worked in.

Steve Bloomer weaved his magic in the Pear Tree area of Derby. He brought joy to his fans and left a lasting legacy to all those that came after him and still continue to support Derby County F.C. For his part in bringing such happiness to my community I always felt he should be given the highest praise, not just because he was a great footballer, but because he was a great man. He was also a father, and in my book no good father should ever be forgotten after they have died. In the process of writing this story I am now able to talk about my own father the way all children should be free to.

I have always known that as long as the memories of people who have passed away are still remembered in the hearts of the living that are left behind then no person will ever truly die. Nobody should ever be forgotten in death, whether they be the father of a Sikh boy from Pear Tree or the father who became one of the greatest footballers the game has ever produced. Steve Bloomer may have achieved a great deal more in his 64 years of life than my father ever did in his 51, but the one thing that unites them is that they were both Pear Tree boys. Something that I will always be proud of and never ashamed of.

By recognising and remembering the legends of our past in my writing I have also been able to restore my father's memory in not only my mind but in all those that knew and loved him too. I did it all for my father and his memory. It has been a long journey to get this far and I have still not stopped travelling, but at least I now know that I have found closure. This closure could only be achieved once I had finally made the decision to prioritise my own personal happiness above any other ambition.

I am the person I am today because of my father. As long as I live I will be proud that Mohinder Singh Dhindsa was my father and that I was raised in the Pear Tree area of Normanton in Derby. I will also be forever appreciative to the destroying angel that showed me the path to happiness.

Without my desire to search for Steve Bloomer, the story of *My Father & The Lost Legend of Pear Tree* would never have been written. Without that, all I would have been left with were my own personal memories and maybe no other wish to keep moving forward and onwards. Steve Bloomer allowed me to share these memories with everyone who reads my story. In my own way I have done what I hoped to always achieve, to make sure that just like Steve Bloomer my father was also never forgotten.

Steve Bloomer inspired me to pursue my dreams. It is because of him that I write. It is because of him that I build statues with Andrew Edwards. It is because of him that I am still here and continue to live my life as a survivor of bereavement by suicide. Steve Bloomer saved my life and made all that possible.

When Steve Bloomer was a child, he was once asked, 'what do you hope to become when you are older?'. Most children who love football would naturally say I want to play for England. Steve Bloomer didn't say that. Steve Bloomer, the little boy from Pear Tree, Derby told the world, 'I'm going to play for England'. And that's exactly what he did.

Some people say that time makes things better. I say that in time you learn to live with your loss better. You never forget, you always feel the loss but the pain is less intense. Why is that? Well it's quite simple. As time goes on the good memories fill the front of your mind and the bad are pushed to the back. Deep down you never forget the pain or the initial loss; you just learn to live with the grief. This is the consequence of loving someone and the price we all pay for love. It still hurts but you have to also accept that as the indirect pain of loss. But remember that the greatest loss can only occur when you forget.

My father's pain is now over. My own personal torment at his passing is now also behind me. These days all I ever think when I remember him are the good times and the memories I still retain. He will live on not only within me but in all those who read my story. Time has been a great healer for me. I just wish I could have reached that point of closure much sooner. But I got there in the end and that is all that matters. I just hope that when people read my story having gone through a similar experience in relation to a loved one that has died by suicide they can reach the point of acceptance much quicker than I ever did.

LIFE AFTER DEATH BY SUICIDE

Since the death of my father I have changed a lot in terms of my character, in some ways good and in some ways maybe not so good – I suppose it depends on how others see me. Before my father's death I was quite diffident. After my father's death and as the years went by I became very much more defiant. An extremity that now defines me as someone who refuses to give up on things that I genuinely believe in and that matter to me. My mental and moral qualities have become quite distinctive to the individual that I am now.

Much of this has manifested itself in my love and strong connection to the city of Derby in which I still live. I only ever want to see the best for my people and it's future. My father's memory is deeply intertwined with that. I want to keep his legacy alive by continuing to help my community and my people when they are in need and they require a voice to speak up and represent them. My father always had difficulties with communicating his thoughts. When I now see people struggling to do the same I refuse to stand back and ignore them. I know that sometimes I might get myself in trouble for sticking my neck out for them, but I choose to do it anyway and carry on regardless. I will always be happy to do this if I believe that the original intentions are good. It is the Sikh way. It is my character. Integrity first. Always. It is the only way I can remain comfortable in my own skin. As my father would always put others first. So, must I. 'I'll do it', as he would always say. But I am also well aware that there are some battles I must not pursue or engage in for my own mental well-being. It's not always about the issue, sometimes it is entirely down to the people you can either trust or not trust. If I engage with something now I have to trust those working with me 100%. If I feel that is not possible then I must walk away. I guess sometimes my father didn't have that ability to disengage, but I have found it's the only way for me to stop myself from falling in the same trap as my father. Loyalty is everything, but sometimes some people will naturally take advantage of your good intentions. For this reason, I have realised that I must also remain firm in my convictions but always uncertain as I know that one-day they may change. That's what life does to you. It can throw so many twists and turns along the way that you must always be ready to adapt to stay alive and survive.

In a sense, I'm reclaiming my past as well as trying to own my future. Control is everything to me now. But I'm also very aware that I should only concern myself with things that I can directly have an affect on or that I can influence. Life is much easier for me to manage this way and a lot more enjoyable to not have the stress of worrying about things that I can't do anything about.

I have done a lot of reading over the last decade. It has helped me a great deal. Reading about people and their lives and realising that we all read to know that we are not alone. Writing has also helped me a great deal. I don't know where I would be without it. My father never had this liberating ability and I know that I would be crippled if I didn't have the written word, but through my words I have allowed his story to also be shared.

In terms of my experiences with suicide I now know that when people are struggling and want to end their lives it is because they truly believe that they have nothing more to expect from life. If only we could intervene at that exact moment and make them realise that life is still expecting something from them. I became fully aware of the importance of this statement when I read *Man's search for meaning* by the Austrian neurologist and psychiatrist Viktor Emil Frankl. I learned a great deal from this wonderful book, which helped me to fully understand what I had been doing for so long without wholly realising.

During my darkest moments I still had dreams of completing my story and one day releasing it as a book. As much as my doubts plagued me, thinking that I might never finish it. I refused to give up and kept pushing myself onwards by telling myself that my story needed to be told and only I could complete it. Nobody else was going to write it for me. I owed that to my father to finish our shared story, to continue to keep his memory alive.

Trying to finish my story gave me a meaning to my own existence, a purpose that had a bearing on my writing as well as all the other creative work I was now involved in such as the creation of statues with my friend, Andy Edwards.
When the possibility of completing my story and releasing my book was finally realised, I was fully able to appreciate the responsibility that I had for my own existence to appear in all its magnitude.

As Viktor Frankl continued to remind me, from that point on I had become conscious of the responsibility I bear not only to my wife and children but also towards my unfinished work, therefore I would never be able to throw my life away. I had found the 'why' for my existence and knew that I could now bear almost any 'how'. It had become my way of showing absolute optimism in the face of adversity – Charhdi Kala as us Sikhs would say.

My father may have died in the most tragic of circumstances, but I believe that my story will continue to allow me to think not of how he died, but how he lived. I have managed to turn my torment and years of suffering into a beneficial human achievement and accomplishment. I have been given the opportunity to change myself for the better. Pain was the motivator for this change in my life, an opportunity to question my life and move on. It became my ultimate motivation, to take responsible action during the time I still have left on this world to make a difference.

However, you want to live your life, first make sure to find your own moral compass and then be true to it. Only then can you appreciate the true meaning of life; to help others find the true meaning in their own lives too.

My original goal has been achieved; from great sadness I have endured and persevered through the darkness.

You never know, when Steve Bloomer's name is mentioned by future generations, the story of the Sikh boy from Pear Tree might also be told.

'Who was that boy?', they might ask.

'Oh, that boy, why, he was the son of Mohinder Singh Dhindsa. He helped the people of Derby reclaim the lost legend of Pear Tree'.

Stephen Bloomer
Mohinder Singh Dhindsa
Kalwinder Singh Dhindsa

All 3 were residents of
Normanton
Pear Tree
Derby
England

Why Raman will always know which team his father supports

Saturday, November 19th 2011 – *The Derby Telegraph*

By Martin Naylor.

A PROUD Derbeian, who was one of the driving forces behind the Brian Clough and Peter Taylor statue at Pride Park, has named his new-born son Raman – after the team he loves.

Kalwinder Singh Dhindsa and wife Ravinder, of Littleover, said that there were a number of reasons behind choosing the name but the main one was the connection of "Ram" to Derby.

Little Raman was born weighing 7lbs 4ozs at Royal Derby Hospital on November 12.

Kalwinder, 32, said: "My main reason for going with it was because of the Derby connection.

"You have the Rams, who I support, of course, and the link with Private Derby, the Swaledale ram, who is the mascot of the 2nd Mercian Battalion, Derby's infantry regiment.

"But another really important reason was that my late father, Mohinder Singh Dhindsa, was originally from a village in Nawanshahr, Punjab, called Ram Rai Pur.

"Obviously, I loved the name Raman and luckily, when we discussed names, my wife liked it from the beginning as well."

Kalwinder, of Breedon Avenue, helped spearhead a campaign for the Clough and Taylor statue which was unveiled outside Pride Park Stadium two years ago.

He met with Ashley Wilkinson, a Littleover Community School pupil who started an online petition for a Brian Clough statue and suggested to him that Peter Taylor also be included.

And, together with cousin Jaz Rai, Kalwinder also designed a Sikh Khanda poppy that was sold for the Royal British Legion's poppy appeal this year.

He felt compelled to create the poppy to mark the 83,000 Sikh soldiers who died during the First and Second World Wars.

He and Ravinder, 30, who works at Derby Crown Court, also have a three-year-old daughter, Layla.

Kalwinder, a wireless web consultant at the Carphone Warehouse, added: "There was one final reason why we chose Raman as a name for our son.

"I have a background in physics and as soon as we discussed Raman as a name I did some searching online and came up with a famous Indian physicist called C.V. Raman, who won a Nobel prize.

"So ultimately there were a number of reasons for choosing the name Raman.

"I wouldn't say Derby County was the main reason but, as Cloughie would have said, it was in the top one!"

Derby County spokesman Matt McCann said the club was delighted at the couple's choice of name for their son.

He said: "It is lovely they've both thought of the connection with Derby and its football club for their son's name and we wish the whole family all the best for the future."

Layla, Rav, Kal and baby Raman next to the statue of Brian Clough and Peter Taylor at Pride Park.

Andrew Edwards

After the unveiling of the Steve Bloomer bust at Pride Park, Andrew Edwards and myself continued our partnership as well as our friendship.

In April 2009, Derby County F.C. announced that they would be erecting a monument to Brian Clough and Peter Taylor at Pride Park. The Clough and Taylor monument was officially unveiled in a family service on Friday, August 27th 2010. I attended the unveiling with Rav and Layla having been personally invited by Derby County F.C.

At this event I was able to meet the families of both Brian Clough and Peter Taylor. Including their wives, Barbara and Lilian respectively as well as all their bairns, except Nigel Clough who was by now the manager of Derby County F.C. and therefore busy preparing for the following day's fixture. Having already obtained Nigel's autograph in Nottingham I then decided to ask for all the family members autographs too, something that many of them had never been asked for until they met me at Pride Park that day. Thankfully they all happily signed on the profile page for their husbands and fathers in my copy of *The Who's Who of Derby County* by

Gerald Mortimer.

Clough and Taylor had finally been reunited – together again.

I also managed to meet another one of my great heroes that day, Dave Mackay. He was accompanied by his wife and daughter. On being introduced to him, he shook my hand and I thanked him for all that he had achieved and contributed to Derby. He also signed his autograph for me. I then told him that he would be next. He took a backward step, shook his head and then began waving his hands from side to side. I looked on puzzled. Oh no, had I offended him? Val, his daughter then leant into him to have a word. She smiled, looked back at me and then repeated what her father had just told her, 'statues are still, they don't move. I was always moving'. 'They could always build you a windmill, Dad', said Val, with a laugh. I smiled in relief, he was quite correct. Dave Mackay was never static. He was dynamic and always moving.

It didn't deter Andy and me though, nor Derby County F.C. On Wednesday, September 2nd 2015, six months after his passing, Isabel Mackay unveiled a 'brick wall bursting' statue to her legendary husband, the late great, Dave Mackay.

Not long after, a statue of Jimmy Sirrel and Jack Wheeler were unveiled at Notts County F.C. after I had recommended Andy to one of the campaign leaders.

Andy and I have worked together on many more statues and monuments since then, as he continues to receive sculpture and statue commissions of national significance as well as increasing international recognition. I personally have one more statue project that I would like to see erected in my home city of Derby within my lifetime.

Kevin Coyne was a musician, singer, composer, film-maker, and a writer of lyrics, stories and poems. The 'anti-star' was born in Derby, England, and died in his adopted home of Nuremberg, Germany.

The fact that he was born in Normanton is of great significance to me but much more important than that is knowing just how much he used his music, art and writing to promote mental health awareness. It can be so disheartening when you try and raise awareness of something close to your heart, but you keep having the doors firmly slammed in your face. This aspect of his music may not have always appealed to the big record companies, but it did not stop Kevin from trying. He never allowed himself to be compromised. He continued relentlessly till the end to get the message out.

My quest for happiness was originally kicked off by Steve Bloomer. It seems quite right that I might just come full circle back to Normanton where it all began. If this is the last statue I ever work on, I'll be more than happy to say I contributed and that I helped bring Kevin Coyne home too.

Kevin Coyne

(Saturday, January 27th 1944 – Thursday, December 2nd 2004)

Steve Bloomer

Thursday, December 15th 2016

Steve Bloomer's England memorabilia sells for £320k. The lot, auctioned in Penzance, Cornwall, was made up of caps, medals and pictures of former England star.

Saturday, January 21st 2017

Real Unión hold a Steve Bloomer Day to pay tribute and mark his birthday. In 1923 Steve Bloomer became the coach of Real Unión in Spain and subsequently guided them to victory in the 1924 Copa del Rey against Real Madrid.

Tuesday, October 3rd 2017

A Derby County XI visit Irun in Spain to contest the first ever Steve Bloomer Trophy in a game against Real Club Irun. A Segunda División B club at their Stadium Gal home.

Friday, February 16th 2018

The Derby Civic Society unveils a blue plaque. The third major memorial in the city to the Rams' most prolific goal-scorer.

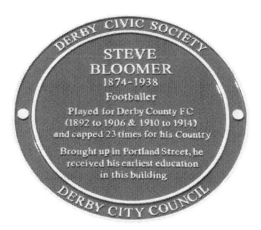

Unveiled on the corner of Pear Tree Street and Portland Street, at his former school building now home to Paul Wallis Fashions.

Thursday, March 22nd 2018

100 Years to the day since Steve Bloomer was released from Ruhleben.

The condition for his release from Germany dictated that he could not immediately return to England to be reunited with his family. Had he done so it would have jeopardised the release of many other older men still in captivity.

Steve Bloomer therefore decided to wait till the end of World War I, only then was he able to eventually complete the long journey home.

Pear Tree – Derby

HONOURS
STEPHEN 'STEVE' BLOOMER
I

FOOTBALL PLAYER

England

British Home Championship Winner

1894–95, 1897–98, 1898–99, 1900–01, 1902–03,[a]
1903–04, 1904–05, 1905–06[b]

British Home Championship Runner-Up

1895–96, 1896–97, 1901–02, 1906–07

a. ^ The title was shared with Ireland and Scotland.
b. ^ The title was shared with Scotland.

Derby County Football Club

Football League First Division Runner-Up

1895–96

FA Cup Runner-Up

1898, 1899, 1903

Football League Second Division Champion

1911–12

HONOURS
STEPHEN 'STEVE' BLOOMER
II

FOOTBALL MANAGER

Real Unión

Campeonato de Guipuzcoa Champion

1923–24

Copa del Rey Winner

1924

HONOURS
STEPHEN 'STEVE' BLOOMER
III

BASEBALL PLAYER

Derby County Baseball Club

British Champion

1895, 1897, 1898

STIGMA OF SUICIDE

In South Asian communities, the man is seen as the head of the household. So much is expected of him from the instant he takes on the responsibility to provide for his family. My father was a proud and gentle man who always tried to do his best for those closest to him. My father was a good man. He was not a criminal; he did not commit a crime. He did not *commit* suicide.

My father, Mohinder Singh Dhindsa, died by suicide on 1st March 2006. My father died from a mental illness that had corrupted his mind, silencing him forever. His death also silenced many more around him who were also deeply affected by his death.

For a long time after his death I tried to avoid using the word suicide. However, when it would slip into conversation I would precede it with commit. In time, I realised that commit was not an appropriate word to use. To commit suicide once upon a time was a crime in this nation before it was abrogated. It is no longer a crime. I refuse to use this term any more as it is not fair on the victims of suicide or their families and loved ones left behind for them to carry this extra burden of implied criminality.

Suicide stops people talking. Whether it is the person who has just taken their own life, or the bereaved loved ones left behind to pick up the pieces. Lack of engagement with the bereaved is a serious problem in the Punjabi community due to the apparent fear of upsetting close family, just not being able to broach the subject, or simply not knowing what to say. Another factor is the issue of shame and dishonour that is deeply instilled in the persona of Punjabi people and their culture. All these factors further diminish the good memories of the loved one who has passed on, and as they are no longer talked about they could be forgotten about forever.

Immediately after my father's death, I knew that I could never allow my memories of him to be lost in time. Therefore, I decided to write down all the feelings and memories I still had of him in my life, up to that point. They had to be written down for posterity; to be kept safe from the fear of one day losing them altogether should my own mind also be corrupted in the same manner as my father's.

Suicide stops people in their tracks. On 1st March, 2006 that was definitely the case for me. It took me a long while to finally get back on track; an uncertain journey that eventually saw me on the straight and narrow. It began almost nine years later when I heard about what led to the death of Robin Williams. The symptoms that he had been experiencing seemed to very much mirror that of my father's – the hallucinations in particular. The phantom aches and pains. As well as his confused state and issues with his memory. I now think of Robin Williams as the man who set me free, the man who provided me with a form of closure and an acceptance of what happened. This freedom gave me the strength to do my utmost to help others who have also travelled a similar path.

It was difficult to talk to anyone at the time; a cloak of silence seemed to have masked all attempts to understand why my father's death occurred. Religion mixed with custom soaked, in culture. Suicide was taboo, a stigma to be avoided at all cost. Eventually, I began to seek some professional help. Thankfully, I was referred to a mental health therapist who helped me set foot on the road to happiness. A person who listened without prejudice, unblemished by society's taboos. Pain was the motivator for my change; an opportunity to question my life and move on. There had been no time to stop and contemplate the darkness. I needed to be distracted. Thankfully writing came to my rescue.

During my darkest moments I still had dreams of completing my story and one day releasing it as a book. As much as my doubts plagued me, thinking that I might never finish it. I refused to give up and kept pushing myself onwards by telling myself that my story needed to be told and only I could complete it. Nobody else was going to write it for me. I owed that to my father to finish our shared story, to continue to keep his memory alive.

(Extract from 'My Father & The Lost Legend of Pear Tree – Part Two')

But what of all those who cannot see a way out, who are not able to communicate their thoughts or feelings, have no energy to engage, no ability to seek help? How do we help them? Anxiety and depression sap their spirit. Suicide will amputate it. Secrets can destroy lives. Especially the lives of those who try to convince the world and themselves that they are not suffering. These people need to know there is no need to hide and that there is a way out if they seek to destroy the stigma of mental illness. There are agencies out there that they can talk to who will understand what they are going through. You are not alone. It's time that our community stopped ignoring the most vulnerable that are obviously in need of help. We need to accept that mental illness corrupts the mind. Let us all take the onus if we see someone in difficulty. We cannot leave it in the hands of those who suffer. We need to show them the light. Help is out there; if only we can help them to access it.

For too long, the Punjabi community has treated mental health issues as a taboo subject. This has resulted in many within our community not being in a position to adequately help all those that experience mental health problems. This stigma needs to be eradicated and confronted head-on by us all. Enough is enough; too many lives have already been destroyed and continue to be devastated because the issue is not dealt with appropriately and effectively. Let's be honest, we all know what mental illness is and the debilitating effects it has on those who experience it. Even though we don't have a word for it in Punjabi, we are all aware of how it makes people behave and feel. Our greatest problem, therefore, is not that we don't have a specific word for depression, but that we don't talk enough about mental illness within our everyday lives.

As a community, many Punjabis follow the Sikh faith. One of the fundamental outlooks in Sikhi is the feeling of always being in a positive mind. The notion of Charhdi Kala 'high rising spirits' – the Punjabi term to aspire to maintain a mental state of eternal optimism and joy. Now, this is a wonderful outlook on life if you are in good health, but it is impossible to accept and live this way if you are going through a serious mental health crisis. Charhdi Kala and prayers alone will not raise the spirits of someone who has found themselves consumed by the darkness of a mental breakdown.

In addition to this, anyone who decides to share their inability to live in Charhdi Kala with others, may themselves become ostracised by the people they confide in as well as the wider community when news leaks out. Many of our own people do not want to be associated with such a negative attitude to life. Some even say that if you can't follow the path of Charhdi Kala, you are not a true Sikh.

Yet, it is the corruption of the mind that makes someone feel so low and dispirited, not a personal choice. In my life, I have come across numerous mental health disorders within our community: anxiety and panic disorders, bipolar disorder, dementia, depression, schizophrenia, and so on.

Each of these are caused by a mixture of biological, psychological, and environmental factors. For example, people who have a family history of mental health disorders may also be more prone to developing one at some point during their lives. Psychological factors and environmental factors, such as upbringing and social exposure, can form the foundations for harmful thought patterns associated with mental disorders. Changes in brain chemistry from substance abuse or changes in diet can also cause mental disorders.

The consumption of alcohol within Punjabi culture is a factor contributing to dual diagnosis of a mental illness and a comorbid substance abuse problem. Punjabi culture has accepted the consumption of alcohol to be a norm; it has been the perceived norm since the mass migration of Indians after the Second World War. This drink culture has been passed down generations without our community ever truly understanding nor accepting the immense harm it does to us all, and especially to those with mental health disorders. This is fundamentally a problem of culture and not Sikhi in general.

Sikhi alone is not going to provide us all with the cure that certain members of our community desperately require. This is not to say we must abandon Sikhi when seeking assistance from mental health professionals. Religious practice can still be integrated with medical expertise, but pursuing a religious lifestyle in the hope that Sikhi alone will cure a mental disorder is an approach that religious leaders must not continue to promote. If this approach continues, I believe we will continue to abandon those that experience the most extreme disorders, by pushing them further into isolation. People with mental health problems need expert medical advice and attention, not be shut away and trapped in their own thoughts.

I know that there are Sikh organisations which combat the issues our community faces regarding mental health issues, and I'm quite sure there are organisations out there that are catering to the Punjabi community, but more needs to be done. Our community needs to direct vulnerable people in the right direction. People with mental health problems and their loved ones need to be provided with information and support from within the gurdwaras and community centres.

Our people are renowned for their strong spirit in times of crisis and adversity. We must now learn to help those among us whose spirit has been broken by the effects of mental illness. We must engage in conversation with all those that have problems and let it be known to them that they are not alone, that we will stand with them, and fight for them. For, is that not the Sikh way?

Let us keep talking. Keep moving on. Keep the faith. Let us disown the stigma of suicide within our community.

This extract can also be found in an anthology called *The Colour of Madness*.

The *Colour of Madness* is a seminal anthology, comprised of poetry, fiction, essays, memoirs and art submitted by BAME writers, academics, mental health workers, artists and those who are still navigating life with mental health problems.

DHINDSA

SPECIAL THANKS

The Derby (Evening) Telegraph

The Post (Sunday Special)

Dave Sudbury

(1987)

'The King of Rome'

(Album, CD)

www.thekingofrome.com

Peter J. Seddon

(1999)

'Steve Bloomer: The Story of Football's First

Superstar'

(Hardcover, Breedon Books)

www.dbpublishing.co.uk

ABOUT THE AUTHOR

Born in Derby in 1979,
Kalwinder Singh Dhindsa attended Village
Community School – a short walk from his childhood
home in Pear Tree. He then graduated from the University
of Leicester with an Honours Degree in Physics with
Astrophysics followed by a PGCE Secondary
Physics.
These days he
works as a science technician
at Littleover Community School.
Life-long member of the Derby Civic Society.